IN THE KING'S PRESENCE

IN THE KING'S PRESENCE

"And the LORD answered me, and said, 'Write the vision, and make it plain upon tables, that he may run that readeth it.'"
(Habakkuk 2:2)

By C.J. Thomas

Second Edition
2 3 4 5 6 7 8 9 10

Published by:
Sharing The Light Ministries, Inc.
P.O. Box 596
Lithia Springs, GA 30122
www.myholycall.com

Library of Congress Catalog Card Number: 95-60986
ISBN 0-9646515-0-5

Printed in the United States of America
First Printing 1995
Second Printing 2005
Third Printing 2010

Acknowledgments:

Cover Photo: Rick Schmidt
Book Photos: Mary Ann Corbitt
Cover Design: Sue Morrissey
Sue Morrissey Art & Design
www.suemartist.com

Sharing The Light Ministries, Inc

Sharing The Light Ministries, Inc.
P.O. Box 596
Lithia Springs, GA 30122
www.myholycall.com

About the Author

C.J. (Cindy) Thomas is an ordained minister, gifted teacher, chief intercessor, and co-founder of Sharing The Light Ministries, Inc. based in Atlanta, Georgia. C.J. is known for sharing the love of Jesus Christ everywhere she goes. ***In The KING'S Presence*** is a collection of inspiring prophetic poetry. In writing this book she has understood the need for transparency. She knew that once a person read the book, in a very real sense, they would know her. At first, she was not too sure she wanted to be *"known"* that well. She was concerned about revealing her heart and especially her human failings, but her heart's desire to be a good steward of the gift of God, has produced ***In The KING'S Presence***. The Lord called her to enter into His presence, know His heart, and share His heart with others. ***In The KING'S Presence*** represents only a small glimpse of her journey of *"growing in grace"*. She knows that as she continues to seek the Lord for His perfect plan for her life, her journey will end in glorious triumph in *"His presence"* in heaven someday!

Special Thanks

I want to give special thanks to my parents, George and Garnet Giles. Your great love and care for me have always inspired me to do my best and allow my life to make a difference in this world. I also want to especially thank C.D. Tompkins and Becky Carr. C.D. saw the vision for ***"In The King's Presence"*** *and encouraged me to share it with the world and she and Becky prayed me through the process. I also want to thank my ministry partner, Sandy Sims, for understanding the prophetic significance of what God wanted to say to the world through these poems. To all of my family and friends, I thank you so much for your love and support. I love you all dearly and praise God for you!*

Introduction

I am dedicating this book of poetry to God the Father, the Lord Jesus Christ, and the precious Holy Spirit. Since I received Jesus Christ as my Lord and Savior, my life has never been the same! I have experienced God's wonderful love and everything else in life pales in comparison!

These poems reflect various seasonal changes in my life. They have inspired, comforted, challenged me, and more importantly revealed to me the **ABSOLUTE** power of God's love.

In order to help you choose a particular poem to read, these poems have been divided into the following subjects:

- **God's Love** has been revealed to my heart by the Spirit of the Lord. He loves me more than I can possibly fathom because He gave His Son for me.

- **Prayer** is my communication with the Lord as well as His communication with me. This time of sharing is vital to my very life and existence.

- **Praise and Worship** offered to the Lord is inspired by His majesty, His holiness, and His love. I respond in praise to His character, attributes, and nature. Worship involves my response to the love relationship I share with my Heavenly Father, Lord Jesus Christ and Holy Spirit.

- **God's Peace** is in the Person of the Lord Jesus Christ, *"The Prince of Peace."* He has protected and comforted me, giving me His peace that passes all understanding. A heart and mind fixed on Him brings perfect peace.

- **God's Purpose** is reflected in all that He does. I began to realize that God is completely committed to His purpose. His purpose, ONLY, will prevail.

- **God's Plan** involves a unique design or pattern for our lives. I received the revelation that God's plan is already blessed. Purposing in my heart to allow Him to establish His plan for my life will bring true fulfillment and joy.

- **God's "Personal" Love** is a collection of words of love and encouragement God gave to me for others.

- **Special Occasions** are the writings of special times and seasons in life.

My prayer is that this book will bless you and transport you....

IN
THE
KING'S
PRESENCE!

Sincerely,
C.J.

THIS IS NOT A SMALL THING THAT YOU HAVE DONE!

I am beginning to understand
That the decisions I make;
Can affect so many lives
For the Kingdom of God's sake.

So many times I have thought,
"Lord, I'm just one person, what can I do;
To make a difference in this
Troubled world, concerning You?"

Sometimes Lord, the burden is so heavy,
I don't want to see anyone lost;
It's then I realize that anything
I can do is definitely worth the cost.

Lord, I'm so glad You got
Your love across to me;
Please use me Lord, that
I might help others to see.

My God said, *"As you have pressed*
Into My presence, at My throne to rest;
The things that have been revealed to your heart,
Certainly include the best.

I have chosen you to know
My heart and you have boldly shared;
You have let others know these things,
Yes, you have made them all aware.

And yes, you are just one person,
But I want you to know;
As you have yielded to Me,
My blessings will flow.

My Child increase your vision,
For there is even more that you can do;
Because it will be My power
And My anointing, that is in you.

As you have been praying for
The Kingdom of God, in your life, to come;
Understand this is not a small thing,
That you have done!"

Reflection: I still find it rather surprising that I should be the author of a book of poetry. I don't recall a particular fondness or leading towards poetry or any other writing. When I penned my first poem, no one was more shocked than I at the result. I regarded it as a singular event, born out of a need for expression. I marveled at how quickly and effortlessly that poem was completed, realizing that I had been moved and directed by the Spirit of the Lord. I was further surprised when my *"one-time"* event began to happen repeatedly. The poems were written quickly and with such ease, there was no doubting that the Lord was the *"Poet"* and I was His poetic vehicle.

This unique collaboration would begin when I was in prayer, meditation, or I desperately needed to cast my cares upon the Lord. Through these experiences, the heart of the *"Most High"* God was revealed to me. At first, I regarded the poems as the Lord's way of blessing me with His very *"personal"* touch and kept them to myself. Then I began sharing them with close friends and others. Many people have told me the poems blessed them and the reflections (a description at the end of each poem as to how and why I wrote it) enhanced their understanding. The Lord gave C.D, my dear friend a heart and vision for this book, which you see reflected in the final result.

At the completion of the smaller first edition of **In The King's Presence,** I read the book and cried. It had been a labor of love, which represented so much of my life. But more than that, I became transparent so that others might see Jesus with me and in me, through all my joys, hopes, dreams, and disappointments. It was *"His Presence"* that made all the difference between victory and failure. C.D., Becky and I prayed that God would use **In The King's Presence** for His glory. That night and several nights afterward, the Spirit of the Lord spoke these words into my spirit; "Cindy, **'This Is Not A Small Thing That You Have Done!'"** To my Lord I give all honor, glory, and praise!

Contents

GOD'S LOVE

"For God so loved the world, that He gave His only begotton Son, that whosoever believeth in Him should not perish but have everlasting life." (John 3:16)

THE CROSS!

Someone came and gave a silver cross to me today.
That he had found one afternoon, while walking along the way.
Though it was somewhat tarnished, it still had great beauty.
And I began to reflect upon its profound significance to me.

I found the cross of Calvary the moment I believed.
The free gift of God, eternal life, I reached out and received.
My spirit was broken when God revealed His love for me.
To my amazement, I saw the Light; it was true reality!

I knew I needed a Savior in the Person of Christ the Lord.
He purchased my salvation at a price I could never afford.
I had always known that Jesus gave His life on Calvary.
But one night it became so personal, I knew He died for me!

Words will never describe the joy I received that night.
The cross became so real to me, I knew that it was right!
Jesus says *"Come take up the cross, follow me, answer the call."*
Because of the love of Christ, the cross is within reach of us all!

Reflection: My oldest brother, Pete, is a beautiful Christian. I will never forget the night that he accepted Christ as his Lord and Savior at a Thanksgiving Eve candlelight communion service. As I saw the tears of repentance, I marveled at the beauty of Christ to change a life the moment a person is born again. My brother has a gift for writing and he uses it for the glory of God. He wrote ***"The Cross"*** as a letter of testimony about an actual experience. I put the letter in the form of a poem. This is his testimony of the power of **"The Cross"** in his life.

A VISION OF MY JESUS

My Jesus, my Jesus, how I love to proclaim;
The love, joy, and peace that accompany that name.
He gave the blind sight and He healed the lame;
Praise be to God Almighty! He is still the same.

I love Him from the very depths of my heart;
Wondering how I ever lived when we were apart.
He touched me with the vision of His death on the cross;
To save a poor sinner like me who was lost.

I could see the horrible stripes He took for my healing;
Oh that this world could see and really start feeling!
I could see the crown of thorns placed on that precious head;
A crown for the King of Kings, Whose precious blood was shed.

I could see the nails driven in His hands and His feet;
And the painful expression on my Savior's face so sweet.
I could hear His plea for forgiveness, a fantastic act of love;
Directed and requested of His Father in heaven above.

His voice rang through the darkness, a cry that it was done;
A cry to a lost and dying world that the Son of God had won!
I could see the jagged spear thrust in His side;
The world thought Him dead, but He will ever abide.

I could see that bloody picture of that day so long ago;
The greatest act of love inspired to win freedom for my soul.
My story has a happy ending because Jesus lives today;
To show those who are earnestly seeking; He's the only way.
He bore my sins and sorrows, my grief, and my strife;
And in addition to all of this, He gave me eternal life.
My precious, precious Savior, draw ever closer to me;
For it was Your wondrous love, that set this captive free.

How wonderful it is to praise and worship the King;
Oh that this entire world would let their praises ring!
Thank You, thank You Jesus, for love incomprehensible;
A debt I can never repay.
You gave me life and love dear Lord;
You are the Life, the Truth, and the Way!

Reflection: This poem is very special to me because it was my first. I remember feeling very low that day. Yet I found myself reflecting upon the great things God had done in my life since I asked Jesus to come into my heart. I began to think about my salvation and the awesome price the Lord Jesus Christ paid for it on Calvary about 2000 years ago. In my mind, I was transported back to the foot of the cross in what I could only describe as **"A Vision Of My Jesus!"**

GUILTY

The verdict has come in on my particular case;
And the judgment it will bring, I must surely face.
The Judge stared at me and said with a pause;
"You were not brought to trial without a cause.
You have broken the law of God and have been found guilty;
In an open examination of facts that you can clearly see."

The Judge, Who is a Holy God, and so full of love and mercy;
Said in a voice marred with pain, *"Sentence: death for eternity."*
I was led away to prison; my prison had no bars.
It did not hide the earth beneath, the sky, the moon or stars.
But nevertheless confining, I was lonely, tormented, and sad,
Wondering can anyone stand before God, or even if anyone had?

But the Judge loved me with a passion, not wanting me to die;
I asked myself over and over, and I still cannot answer why.
He said, *"I want to save you, but my justice I must satisfy;*
You see I Am the Eternal God, not a man that I should lie."
He said, *"In order for the wages of sin to repay;*
One must die in your stead, that is the only way.

Someone Who is righteous and upright before me;
Can save you and allow Me to grant mercy.
Since it's impossible for one like you to overcome sin;
I will send my only Son as a man, and the battle He will win.
He will take your burden of sin, My anger, and My wrath;
And to reconcile the two of us, faith in Him will be your path.

The verdict in your case has changed from guilty to innocent;
And can change for every soul; for this cause My Son was sent.
Because of the life and death of the only Righteous One;
Who is My pride, My joy, and My only begotten Son.
You have now received a pardon that is completely full and free;
The adoption as My Child, and eternal life; your destiny!"

Reflection: As I continued to grow in the Lord through His Word, I began to see the personality and the very nature of God. The Bible beautifully reveals the heart and mind of Almighty God. It seemed that I first saw Him as my loving Heavenly Father as Jesus describes Him in the gospels. Then I realized that He is indeed the Judge of all heaven and earth. I also realized that before I accepted my salvation, He was my Judge and His verdict for me was **"Guilty."** Now that I have received the Lord Jesus Christ as my personal Savior, my guilt changed to innocence and my Judge became my loving Heavenly Father!

WHAT IS LOVE?

Since time immemorial, this question has been pondered;
Each of us at one time in our lives has wondered.
One day I found the answer in the depths of my being;
A truth so glorious and wonderful, I couldn't help seeing!

A startling view of loneliness and emptiness inside;
In a particular size and shape, such that *"Someone"* could abide.
I wondered, *"How can I fill this inner desolation;*
That people have no doubt experienced since creation?"

No sooner had I asked this question, quickly the answer came;
I heard the Lord's still small voice; He even knew my name!
He said, *"I created you and of this void I am very much aware;*
And I am here to heal that desolation, lack, and despair.

You see I fit perfectly in that void space in your heart;
Because that is the way I made you right from the start.
If you sincerely ask Me, I will be more than happy to come in;
Together there's nothing we can't do, for we will always win.

And you will cease to wonder about this question of love;
The answer will be crystal clear once you are born from above.
Because you see I am Love; therefore everything you need;
And because I loved you, in others you will plant this seed.

You will tell them how I loved them so;
And I gave My only Son just to let them know.
He broke down that wall of sin that separated Me from you;
And did everything a Father like Me could ask His Son to do.

Tell them My Son's death was filled with untold grief and pain;
And the question that faces them is; will His death be in vain?"
Now about this question: What is love? I can now clearly see;
I can tell this world without a doubt, that *"Love"* lives in me!

Reflection: I have the most wonderful family in the world! You must realize that I am slightly prejudice! As I was growing up, I always had that sense of well being, knowing that God had especially blessed me with a family that loved me. I thought I knew all about love, but my greatest lesson was yet to come. I met the Lord Jesus Christ and in Him, I found a love so true and so complete, and the capacity to love others in a way that I never knew existed before. My initial ideas about love were vastly different from what I experienced in God. So, I decided to pose the vital question, **"What is Love?"**

GOD'S PECULIAR TREASURE!

Lord, I'm amazed at Your power and greatness;
Yet in my life, I see Your personal touch.
It's so wonderful to know a God so big;
Could love little me so much!
The revelation of Your love; is growing inside of me each day.
As You keep confirming Your Word; I clearly hear You say:

*"Today if you will promise; to hear and obey My voice.
And keep My Word, you will; have reason to rejoice.
You are a chosen vessel; surrender to Me your all.
Consider what David said in Psalms; listen and recall.
You're fearfully and wonderfully made; you will find,
You are extraordinary; you are one of a kind.
No one can do the things; I have called you to do,
And the task I have for each; is just as special too.*

*And this truth in your heart; I want to be revealed.
It's wonderful and glorious; not to be concealed.
Do you know that you are special;
And you bring Me much pleasure?
You are unique; you shall be called;
God's peculiar treasure!"*

Reflection: I was talking to a dear friend of mine one night. At the end of the conversation, she told me that she considered herself to be *"God's Peculiar Treasure."* That phrase touched my spirit, so I looked up the scriptures that contained the phrase. I found that I too am considered to be God's *"purchased prized possession!"* Praise God! At that moment, I became so aware of the power and majesty of my Lord and so grateful that the God of the universe had chosen me. Our Heavenly Father created us for His pleasure and He began to reveal to me how special we are to Him. He showed me that I am also **"God's Peculiar Treasure"** and so are you if you have been born again and purchased by the Blood of Jesus Christ!

A PRECIOUS GEM

I have found I need a special love in life to pull me through;
A love so deep and precious; a love that's really true.

A jewel and grateful possession, I would be to Him;
My deepest desire is to be Someone's precious gem.

I found no one to love me, with a love so true;
I searched and searched, and I didn't know what to do.

I was deeply saddened by this, feeling so very, very empty;
Suddenly I realized only *"Perfect Love"* could fulfill me.

I found human love to be lacking in so very many ways;
But Praise God, His love is sufficient, for all of our days!

Rarely is human love given unconditionally and free;
But there's nothing that compares to God's love, grace, and mercy.

If no one loves me, this I know that Jesus loves me; and to Him;
I'm special, I'm important; I'm His precious gem!

Reflection: This particular day, I was feeling neglected, unloved, and somewhat disappointed in human nature. There are so many people who are feeling lonely. Perhaps they have no family or loved ones, or have been hurt and disappointed by human failings. I feel so blessed to know that there is nothing like the love of God! His love is something I can always count on. It's wondrous, unconditional, and eternal! I'm so glad He belongs to me and I belong to Him, and praise God; I am His **"Precious Gem!"**

WHO LOVES YOU MORE?

I heard my Father say, in a soft sweet gentle voice;
"I have something to say, which should cause you to rejoice.
I have so much to give you, so much good in store;
Just ask yourself the question Child, Who loves you more?
Open up your eyes, just look around and see;
Every good and perfect gift, comes from Me.

When things happen to you, that you do not understand;
You question My love for you, and all of My plans.
The circumstances are before you, and it's all you seem to see;
Listen, I will be responsible, just turn it over to Me!
When you don't understand why things happen as they do;
Trust Me, I will perfect everything concerning you.

To the truths taught in My Word, Child you must yield;
Did I not say My truth, will be your buckler and your shield?
Cast your cares upon Me, and I will set you free;
Please purpose in your heart, you'll put your faith in Me.
Again I say, I have so much to give you, so much good in store;
Just ask yourself the question My Child, Who loves you more?"

Reflection: I had just suffered a major disappointment. As I was contemplating my pain and wondering how I would ever recover from it, the Spirit of the Lord asked me, *"Cindy, Who loves you more?"* Somewhat startled, I replied; *"No one Lord, no one loves me as much as You do".* As a point of truth, no one can possibly love us more perfectly in every way than God does. He is *"Love"* and His love always seeks our highest good. It is all encompassing and eternal in its scope. He then began to give me a word that has served to sustain me throughout all the trials and challenges that have come and those that are yet to come. Each time I am tempted to question His love for me and His concern for my well being, I remember His question to me that day; **"Who Loves You More?"**

I'LL BE WAITING FOR YOU!

Dear loved one there is something that is on my heart,
I hardly know how to say it, or even how to start.
I have to make you understand just how much there is at stake;
There's a date you must keep with me; one you cannot break!

I want you to promise, that no matter what this life may bring;
That you will keep this date, because to me, it's everything!
No matter how rich, famous, or successful you may someday be;
Don't let anything stand in your way, it's very important to me!

I just want to be sure that with me, you will keep this date;
I promise to meet you just inside heaven's eastern gate.
My prayers and intercession shall not be in vain, that's true;
Please don't forget to meet me there; I'll be waiting for you!

Now please don't disappoint me, and say that you will not come;
Our way has been made, through Christ Jesus the Son.
When we ask Christ into our heart, our miracle has begun;
His love has made the difference, and the battle has been won!

Eternal life is promised, the Lord imparts it as our own;
Throughout all the endless ages, God's heaven will be our home.
When I see you there, my bottled prayers and tears I'll show.
You will realize my love for you, my God, at last you'll know!

So I just need to be sure that with me, you will keep this date;
I promise to meet you just inside, heaven's eastern gate.
My prayers and intercession shall not be in vain, that's true;
Please don't forget to meet me there; I'll be waiting for you!

Reflection: My sister-in-law related a story to me about a Christian parent asking his child to please make the decision to ask Christ into his heart so that they could meet in heaven someday. As she related the story to me she said that it would make a lovely poem. She also said that she felt certain that the Spirit of the Lord would give me this poem. A few nights later, I was awakened in the middle of the night with thoughts of my unsaved loved ones. There was an overwhelming desire to somehow make them understand how much God loved them and how much I loved them. I began to tell them; **"I'll Be Waiting For You!"**

PRAYER

**"And when He had sent them away,
He departed into a mountain to pray."
(Mark 6:46)**

IF YOU WILL NOT QUIT; YOU CANNOT LOSE!

"Know that I Am the Lord, and just be still.
One place you want to be, is in My will.

You must have an open communication with Me.
Spending time in daily prayer, that is the key.

It's one thing to read the Word and say 'Amen that's true.'
But you must truly believe My Word will work for you.

Pray; 'Lord give me this day my daily bread.'
You are to pray like Jesus did; take note of what He said.

You must sow your words, as if you were planting seeds.
Be specific in your asking and tell Me your daily needs.

Be tenacious, I'll not be mocked; My promise I will keep.
Because whatsoever you shall sow, you shall also reap.

All that I have is yours, but Child you must choose.
If you will not quit, you simply cannot lose!"

Reflection: I was in church one night listening to a dynamic teaching. The minister outlined four points in receiving from God and getting your needs met. They were: *1) Be in the will of God; 2) Believe God's Word will work for you; 3) Be specific in your asking; 4) Be tenacious, don't quit.* The next day while in prayer, the Lord gave me these points in the form of this poem. He was telling me personally that there was much that He wanted to give me, but the choice was mine. He said; **"If You Will Not Quit, You Cannot Lose!"**

I WILL BE WHATEVER YOU NEED ME TO BE!

"Look to Me dear one; realize I Am your key.
I will be whatever you need Me to be!

I Am Yahweh Tsidkenu; your righteousness.
I love you My Child; I would say that you are blessed.

I Am Yahweh M'kaddesh; I have sanctified you.
And will free those from sin, who will accept Me too!

I Am Yahweh Shalom; I give you peace that will last.
And My will for your life; I will bring it to pass.

I Am Yahweh Shammah; The Ever Present One.
I'm with you in the night, sunrise, and with each setting sun.

I Am Yahweh Rophe; I Am the Lord that healeth thee.
I made complete provision for you; spirit, soul, and body.

I Am Yahweh Jireh; I provide, I'm the One Who sees.
Look to Me to meet your needs; I Am all sufficient for thee.

I Am Yahweh Rohi; I Am your Shepherd, please take heed.
Because the Lord is your Shepherd, you have all that you need.

I Am Yahweh Nissi; your banner, I'm your security.
My angels surround you daily; they have charge concerning thee.

Look to Me dear one; please realize I Am your key.
I will always be whatever in life, you need Me to be!"

__Reflection:__ *"Our Father which art in heaven, hallowed be thy name."* I was learning to hallow or consecrate the name of the Lord by using the Hebrew redemptive names of Yahweh or God the Father. At that moment, He spoke to my heart and said**, "I Will Be Whatever You Need Me To Be!"** What do you need Him to be in your life today? If you need Him to be your Lord and Savior, please pray this prayer: *"Dear Heavenly Father, I come to you in the name of Your Son, the Lord Jesus Christ. I repent of my sins and I ask Your forgiveness. I believe Jesus died for my sins and that You raised Him from the dead. I'm asking You now Jesus, to come into my heart and become Lord and Savior of my life. I realize at this moment that I am born again and will live for You all the days of my life. Thank You Lord for saving my soul! Amen."*

WHOM DO YOU SAY THAT I AM?

Building my faith is what my Lord is sharing with me;
Because I need revelation; yes my God, I want to see!

He said, *"Listen to Me Child, this is what you must do;*
Because whom YOU say that I Am, is what I will be to you!

I Am your Lord and Savior, you must confess that Jesus is Lord;
My power overshadows you, with heart and mind in one accord.

I Am the Alpha and Omega, your beginning and your end;
Confess that in your life, I Am truly your best friend.

In the Lord Jesus, you always triumph and have victory;
Confess that I Am your success, and then allow Me to be.

You need a miracle, your miracle worker I Am this day;
Confess this about Me, and watch how I will make a way!

I Am your healer, understand and claim your goal;
Confess that I Am the only One, Who can make you whole.

I Am the One Who is worthy, of all your praise;
With the fruit of your lips, My name you will raise.

I Am your love giver, the very lover of your soul;
Confess how much I love you, and give Me complete control.

I Am the restorer of your soul, because I Am your peace;
Confess that I bring peace and joy, and it never has to cease.

Again I say My Child, this is what you must do;
Because whom YOU say that I Am, is what I will be to you!"

Reflection: I was reading Matt. 16:15-18 one day. Jesus asked Peter the question, *"Whom say ye that I Am?"* Peter made the awesome statement, *"Thou art the Christ, the Son of the living God."* On the rock of that confession the Lord Jesus Christ has built His Church, of which the gates of hell cannot prevail against. The Spirit of the Lord began to deal with me, asking me; *"Whom do you say that I Am?"* Ultimately every person will face an encounter with the risen Lord and will be, in effect, asked that same question. Our response to this question, like Peter's, will have far reaching implications concerning this present life. And more importantly, it will affect our eternal life. The Lord was telling me that ***He would be to me whatever I confessed Him to be, according to His Word***. In other words, He is the All Sufficient One, the God Who is more than enough to meet every need in every circumstance in my life. The question faces me every day; **"Whom Do You Say That I Am?"**

ARE YOU WILLING TO *PRAY* THE PRICE?

The Lord my God spoke to my heart today;
"I have something to ask you, something to say.

Is praying for others a desire of your heart?
If that is not true, that's where we must start.
Next there must be an element of discipline in your life;
This will help you to avoid so much sorrow and strife
Then into My presence is where you will find delight;
It is then you will know everything will be all right
You know, the call to prayer, is the highest call of all;
Many don't realize this, that's why they stumble and fall.
In My Word, I said for you to count the cost;
Tell Me, will you spend time in prayer for the lost?

You say you are saved and on your way to heaven, that's nice;
But for some lost soul, are you willing to pray the price?"

Reflection: One of the most depressing portions of scripture I have ever read is Ezek. 22:30-31. The Lord is saying that He sought for someone to stand in the gap, to repair the opening or breach in the wall - that gap between man and God, but found no one. *"Standing in the gap"* is a type of committed intercession. It is so startling to realize that God is saying, that if He could have found one person to stand before Him and intercede, judgment could have been avoided. The intercessor always comes to God on *"behalf of others"*, to repair the *"break"* in the wall. While restoring the damaged wall, the intercessor also plugs or covers up that *"gap"* against the enemy. When I would read this scripture, my heart would ache and in my heart I would say to the Lord; *"You don't have to look for me, I'm here!"* I said yes to my Lord when He asked me personally, **"Are You Willing To *Pray* The Price?"**

THE GIFT OF GIVING

God the Father had a heartfelt need;
In response to this, He planted seed.

God wondrously loved this world so;
He gave Christ the Son to let them know.

A harvest of children, He expected to reap;
To live eternally with Him; to keep.

And God's example in giving, I'm to follow His lead;
And show others my Jesus can meet every need.

My desire is to show His love, and to share;
That God gave to me, love beyond compare.

And I don't want to just give money or wealth;
Help me dear Lord; give more and more of myself.

I know only one way to really start living;
I'm asking, *"Lord, please, give me the gift of giving!"*

Reflection: I cried when I heard of a situation where someone I knew was sick and in the hospital. I also knew she was feeling confused and completely abandoned and unloved. I thought; *"She could have a great sum of money, but it wouldn't mean as much as knowing someone really loved her."* I'm so glad that despite the trials of life, I have a blessed hope and full assurance that if no one loves me, my God does! But that night, my heart went out to her and those like her who don't realize that God loves them. I asked God to allow me to give myself to her in prayer. Actually, I was asking God to give me **"The Gift Of Giving!"**

MY TIMES AND MY SEASONS ARE IN YOUR HAND!

My Father and my God, my prayer I speak to You this day;
I want Your purpose in my life, for there's no better way.
In times past, You have come and revealed Yourself to me.
Your hand has been upon my life; I have seen this reality.
Lord, I have felt so warmed and protected by Your love;
Knowing that every good and perfect gift comes from above.

I hear the voice of Your Spirit; Your words are mine to keep;
"The future is before you now, it's the time and season to reap!"
Although there are many things I have yet to understand;
My God, I know my times and my seasons are in Your hand!

Father, I'm so glad that I gave my heart and life to you;
And You show me that Your heart and life are all mine too!
And I am confident that You have begun a good work in me;
And will perform it until the day of Christ, this I clearly see.
In Your Word, I see that everything has its time and its season;
You established seedtime and harvest; that is the reason.

I hear the voice of Your Spirit; Your words are mine to keep;
"The future is before you now, it's the time and season to reap!"
Although there are many things I have yet to understand;
My God, I know my times and my seasons are in Your hand!

Reflection: Our lives are a series of times and seasons. In Genesis, the Lord established seedtime and harvest. Everything in life works according to this principle. There is a time of planting seed and eventually there will be a harvest. The Word of God tells us that we reap the kind of harvest according to the type of seed that we have sown. It is vitally important to sow that which is good and pleasing in the Lord's sight so we can reap a bountiful harvest of blessings. This poem was an acknowledgement of His love and presence in my life, and also that I needed to submit to the Lord's timing in regard to my seasonal development. I understood that and began to say to my Lord, "**My Times And My Seasons Are In Your Hand**!"

FEED ME UNTIL THERE IS NO MORE LACK IN ME!

The heart cry of my spirit, my Lord, only You can see;
Feed me until, there is no more lack in me!

You said, *"I Am the bread of life, come from heaven above;"*
You freely invite everyone to eat, and partake of all Your love.
So I will enter into Your presence and behold Your face;
Yes, I will spend my quiet time in the Secret Place.
As I behold Your face, I will change as I see Your glory;
And the Spirit of the Living God, will set my spirit free.
Those areas in me that are incomplete, the Holy Spirit will show;
All the lack inside of me will be filled; praise God, it has to go!
Lord, You are the *"Source of all life,"* for time and eternity;
And I must continually feed on You, or there'll be no life in me.

This heart cry of my spirit, my Lord, only You can see;
Please feed me until there is no more lack in me!

Reflection: The theme of the program was *"Feed Me Until I Want No More"*. I was one of the main speakers and the Lord confirmed the theme with this poem. I began to think of John 6:32-35, and the truth the Lord gave when He revealed He was the *"True Manna"*, the Bread of Life, come down from heaven. If anyone was to have life, they must feed on Him. Feeding continually on Jesus will bring completeness to every part of our being. To feed on Him means to spend time in His presence and renew our minds (soul) with the Word of God. II Cor. 3:18 reveals that we are changed from glory to glory. As our spirits are set free to soar into His presence, we are supernaturally changed into His image by whatever level of His glory we are able to behold. In other words, we will reflect what we see! My heart cry to the Lord was for this completeness in my life; to be like Him. I asked the Lord to **"Feed Me Until There Is No More Lack In Me!"**

IT IS TIME TO PLEASE THE KING!

Sweet Spirit, I want to know You, in a very special way;
I want to love You and feel Your presence Lord, every day.
I know You want to reveal to me, the Father and the Son;
So with everything within me, I will understand that we are one.
Precious Spirit, I need You, to become all that I should be;
For without Your love and guidance, my Lord, I just can't see!
Holy Spirit is speaking to my heart; right now I hear it ring;
"It is time, it is time, it is time to please the King!"

Just wanting to be more like You Lord, my battle is all but won;
As I love You with all of my heart; Your kingdom has to come!
Your finished work on Calvary was designed to set me free;
To bring me to the place You made, of total victory.
Being in that place, is the overwhelming cry of my heart,
As my spirit forms the image inside, my words to You will start;
This prayer that will become to You my heart's love offering;
"Yes, it is time, it is time, it is time to please the King!"

Reflection: I was listening to a sermon. I can't tell you what the message was about. I only know that the Spirit of the Lord chose to highlight one phrase that was said during the message - I heard it said; ***"It is time to please the King!"*** Right away my spirit was energized and in that service I began to write these words. The Holy Spirit does indeed search our hearts and questions our true motivations. My life at that time, although I was not consciously aware of it, could be characterized as *"quiet rebellion."* I had experienced devastating losses in my life. I appeared to be all right on the outside, but on the inside I was a fractured human being. In my human reasoning, I felt that I would never experience *"wholeness"* in my emotions again. But the Love of my life, my Lord, touched my heart and emotions that day as I penned this prayer. The Spirit of the Lord wanted to heal and bring me to the place where I would say with resolve in my heart; **"It Is Time To Please The King!"**

DO YOU HAVE A SPECIAL BLESSING JUST FOR ME?

My precious loving Father, I make my appeal to You this day;
I simply need to experience Your love for me, in a special way.
My soul is fainting; my heart is sorrowful and heavy;
And the shadows of the past seem to be overtaking me.

Yet as I step into Your glorious light, flowing from above;
Driving back the shadowy darkness, with Your matchless love.
I see You as full of grace and mercy, and this is my key;
So I ask Lord, *"Do You have a special blessing just for me?"*

As I look back across the scenes of my life gone by;
I sit here, and I wonder, and I begin to question why.
Why am I in this particular place in my life?
And Lord God, why is there so much confusion and strife?

I don't have the answers to these questions, that is for sure;
And for the pain I feel right now, within myself, I have no cure.
But You are full of grace and mercy, and this is my key;
So I ask Lord, *"Do You have a special blessing just for me?"*

Oh God, there were just so many lost and wasted years;
As I think about it now, my eyes grow wet with tears.
But dwelling on the past is not what my heart should gauge.
My future is an open book, and I can write a brand new page!

And Lord I know that You're with me, surely this I know;
You promised to never leave me; You said You would never go.
I make a demand upon Your grace and mercy, for this is my key;
I ask again Lord, *"Do You have a special blessing just for me?"*

Reflection: My life had changed drastically in a very short period of time. I was reaping the harvest of some wrong decisions I had made in my life. Even though I understood that my Lord is a God of *"new beginnings"*, I was desperately trying to deal with past issues. The problem was that *"I"* was dealing with them instead of giving them to my faithful and loving Lord. Through my pain, I began to focus on two characteristics of my Lord. Not only is He full of grace and mercy, He indeed personifies *"Grace"* and *"Mercy."* I have found that His grace and mercy can outlast anything that has happened or will ever happen in our lives. His answer for me was *"Yes!"* as I asked Him; **"Do You Have a Special Blessing Just For Me?"**

NOBODY BUT JESUS IS GOING TO RUN MY LIFE!

I declare this today, no more confusion and strife;
Nobody but Jesus is going to run my life!

Come Kingdom of God, in my life today;
I'm putting my foot down, that's how I will pray.

This day Lord I say; *"In my life, Thy will be done;"*
I will say it again Lord God, *"Kingdom of God, come!"*

The Kingdom of God will surely come, in my family;
I'm saying; *"I shall not be moved";* that is the key.

The Kingdom of God will come in the Body of Christ too.
Spending time in prayer is what we all must do.

The Kingdom of God will have to come in this nation of mine.
A great spiritual awakening, revival; it's about time!

I declare this today, no more confusion and strife.
Nobody but Jesus is going to run my life!

Reflection: I heard a minister say ***"Nobody but Jesus is going to run my life."*** The words were powerful and anointed and went deep into my spirit. The very concept that God wants His Kingdom to come and His will to be done on earth as it is in heaven is awesome. John 10:10 states that Jesus came to give us *"abundant life."* With His life, death, resurrection, and glorification, Christ purchased our right (authority) to tap into the Kingdom of God, with all of its benefits. I decided to make a demand upon the finished work of my Lord Jesus Christ by declaring; **"Nobody But Jesus Is Going To Run My Life!"**

I JUST WANT TO TALK TO YOU!

"I wake you each morning, as you get your start.
And I gauge every thought that is in your heart.
I wonder if you're thinking of fellowship; just us two.
I know that's My heart cry; I just want to talk to you.

All too often, It's sad to say; I feel a little empty.
Your very first thoughts in starting your day are sadly not of Me.
Your life is important to Me, and you know that is true.
So why limit your time with Me; I just want to talk to you.

Morning, noon, and night, I seem to wait for your cry;
Of praise, of love; but I don't hear and I begin to wonder why.
I love you and I created you to love Me too.
I have waited so long; I just want to talk to you!"

My Lord and my Love; I'm so grateful for cleansing from sin.
I can't express my gratitude for Your great love that took me in.
Forgive me Lord, I'm forgetful, I'm made of flesh.
My God, You understand that is true.
But please believe me when I tell You Lord;
My joy is only complete when I'm privileged to talk to You!

Reflection: Our lives are so busy sometimes and there doesn't seem to be enough hours in the day to accomplish everything. But I found that we must order our lives and set the right priorities. The Lord Jesus commended Mary for choosing the *"good part;"* to sit at His feet, absorb His words and enjoy His presence. He cautioned Martha not to be so caught up in the cares of this life, missing the *"good part."* I was moving into a new house. There was so much work, preparation, and time involved. I wasn't spending much time with the Lord until He spoke to my heart one day; **"I Just Want To Talk To You!"**

PRAISE AND WORSHIP

"But the hour cometh, and now is, when the true worshipers shall worship the Father in spirit and in truth: for the Father seeketh such to worship Him."
(John 4:23)

WHO IS LIKE UNTO THE LORD? (PSALM 113)

Who is like unto the Lord our God, Who dwells on high?
Praise Him heaven and earth; lift your hands to the sky!
Praise the Lord; praise Him all you servants of the Lord.
Lift up your voice, bless His name in one accord.
Bless Him from this time forth and for evermore.
Sing high praises like you've never sung before!

He is truly worthy to be praised, so let's exalt His name;
From the rising of the sun to the going down of the same.
And as for the nations, the Lord Most High is above them all.
Heaven and earth speak of His glory; can't you hear the call?
The things in heaven and earth, He humbles Himself to behold.
No one compares to my Lord, He's more precious than gold!

Out of the dust He lifts up and exalts the needy and the poor.
That He may set them with princes, not to be downcast anymore.
God gives the barren woman a wonderful house to keep.
She is a joyful mother of children, with blessings to reap.
Who is like unto the Lord our God, Who dwells on high?
Praise Him heaven and earth; lift your hands to the sky!

Reflection: One morning I was reading Psalm 113. 1 got so caught up in the beauty and majesty of my Lord. It's a wonderful praise psalm and as I read it, I could identify with the Psalmist as he details why our God is so worthy to be praised! There is truly no one like the Lord! When you really know Him, you can see His sweet nature, mercy, power, and His majesty. I stand amazed in His presence and eternally grateful that I belong to Him! This particular morning, like the Psalmist, I asked; **"Who Is Like Unto The Lord?"**

I'LL NEVER FORGET WHAT YOU HAVE DONE FOR ME!

Lord, I want and need to praise You everyday;
Living in Your presence daily is the only way.
Not just picking and choosing times, I don't know when;
Continual praise is to be offered, not just now and then.

Lord, You were the spotless Lamb sacrificed on the cross;
To give hope and freedom to all who are lost.
You took the sins of the entire world; behold the Lamb;
God in the flesh, overflowing with love, yes, behold the man!

Heaven and earth marveled at how far the Father would go;
And Your wonderful obedience to Him, to let mankind know.
The awesome price the Father paid to redeem us from sin,
So that we might know the beauty of being born again.

My life never made sense, until You entered in;
To show me a better way, with freedom from sin;
And because I have never experienced love so true;
Living my life to please You is what I must do.

I just wanted to take the time to tell You today;
That I love You Lord, and forever I will say;
I will give to You praise, honor, and glory, You see;
Because I will never forget what You have done for me!

Reflection: I had just watched a movie depicting the life of Christ. As I watched the scenes of torment and the actual crucifixion, I thought to myself, *"He loved me so much; He did all of that for me!"* The plan of redemption was so glorious that heaven and earth marveled as it was unfolding. I just wanted to tell my Lord that I personally understood the sacrifice that He made to redeem me. I told Him, **"I'll Never Forget What You Have Done For Me!"**

HOW MUCH I AM BLESSED!

It is so easy to grumble and complain;
But I want to praise God in sunshine and rain.
It's easy to see the sin and confusion around;
Instead of our God's grace, which much more abounds.
So many love evil instead of good;
But the Word of God says that not all would.

There are those who want darkness instead of light;
But praise God for those who want what is right!
Most people choose to look at the negative side;
But there is a positive, upon this I decide.
I don't want to be like all of the rest;
Father, help me to see how much I am blessed!

The things that are pure and lovely, I want to see;
Remembering God's blessings, that's the key.
I know when I take the time to look around;
There are so many of God's blessings to be found.
The greatest blessing is the price Jesus paid for me;
When He shed His precious blood, and died on Calvary.

Remembering this, I will always be conscious of;
My God's wonderful, constant, and abiding love.
But this world is blind, they take for granted God's mercy;
But I will shout about it now, and throughout eternity.
I don't want to be like all of the rest;
Father, help me to see how much I am blessed!

Reflection: I was overwhelmed with the thought of all of the blessings God had placed in my life. Oh, I had problems all right, but I chose to focus on my blessings. Have you ever been around people who seem to be negative all of the time? They rarely see the good things in life. I purposed in my heart that I don't ever want to be like that. At this season in my life, I decided to take the time to remember just **"How Much I Am Blessed!"**

LET GOD BE MAGNIFIED!

One day in my heart, I began to pray;
"Lord, I need your guidance, please show me the way.
Everything in my life, is falling apart right now;
I want to make things right, but I just don't know how.
Things look very grave indeed, and I just want to shout;
Let me off this crazy world, I want to get out!"
But in my prayer, I began to submit myself to You;
Wondering when I would hear my answer, and what I must do.

My head was confused, but in my spirit a light began to shine;
Your Word opened to me, and I knew everything was fine.
In Your Word, David said; *"O magnify the Lord with me;"*
And I agreed that is the way it should always be!
It also says; *"Let's exalt His name together, in one accord";*
You're the God of heaven and earth; the only Lord!

So I asked Lord how can I magnify You, in all that I do?
I hear; *"Child think less of the power, that things have over you.*
Think more of My power, that is in you to succeed;
The battle is Mine, and you know I've won the victory!"
So I placed the truth of God's Word, in my heart that day;
Knowing that His Word will always enlighten my way.
And in my heart the declaration formed and my spirit cried:
"No matter what things look like, let my God be magnified!"

Reflection: Have you ever been in a situation where the most precious and important things in your life seem to be falling apart? In those times, you feel so helpless. You search for answers and there doesn't seem to be any. The Bible teaches that the Christian should face trials with overcoming praise. If we send Judah (Praise) first, our battle will be won. We send up praises to Almighty God and He will fight our battles. My God is worthy to be praised, worshiped, and adored! Praise His Wonderful Name! The circumstances in this life don't always cooperate with us. But one thing is certain - God is still worthy of our praise, so **"Let God Be Magnified!"**

PRAISE HIS HOLY NAME!

Father, I know that You know the pain that is in my heart;
The pain is real and deep, and it is tearing me apart.
My feelings and emotions have been shattered and abused.
I wonder what I did to deserve this; I'm so hurt and confused.
Sometimes it seems, out of life I ask for far too much;
Yet I know that what I need, is Your strong yet gentle touch.
I know that my hope deferred, has made my heart sick;
A tree of life is promised; I wish my desire would come quick!

When trials came, David encouraged himself in the Lord,
Because he knew that the loss of joy, he could not afford.
And I hear You telling me Lord, that I will never be the same;
Once I move into Your presence and praise Your Holy Name!
Lord I know, that for me to grumble and complain, is sin;
But it's hard to see the end, even though I know that I win.
Your Word says that I am to give thanks in everything;
And to count it all joy, in trials, and let my praises ring.

I guess that is why You call it the sacrifice of praise;
It will cost me everything; I have to change my ways.
And my Lord said,

"My Child, My joy will be to you, a saving grace;
Lift up your head and praise Me, I want to see your face.
I tell you, the joy of Your Lord will come and overshadow you;
There will be others affected by this anointing on you too.
Believe Me, My Child when I tell you,
You will never be quite the same;
When you move into My presence
And begin to praise My Holy Name!"

Reflection: One night while in praise service, I had a decision to make. My mind was focusing on how hurt my feelings were. I wanted to just break down and cry. I knew that I should enter into praise and allow God to lift me up, but I was wavering. A dear friend of mine said to me at that moment that God was showing her all of the pain in my heart. She then told me that she loved me and encouraged me to enter into praise. Praise God for our brothers and sisters in Christ! Joy is a major spiritual force. The joy of the Lord is our strength. There are times in life when we must make a decision to give God the sacrifice of praise, even when we don't feel like it. God showed me that night that I would never be the same once I had made my decision, in spite of circumstances, to **"Praise His Holy Name!"**

EXCEPTIONAL PRAISE AND WORSHIP!

"Understand don't be overcome
With this life and its pleasures;
Because I have more for you;
For where your heart is, there's your treasure.
I'm inviting you to step out of the normal routine;
If you want to experience things that are rarely seen.
Giving to Me continuous praise, My glory you will see;
When exceptional praise and worship is offered unto Me!

When you bring the evening sacrifice of worship and of praise;
Purpose in your heart, the name of the Lord you will raise.
'The Lord is good and His mercy
Endures forever;' you will say;
'You redeemed me from the enemy's hand,
Lord I thank you this day!'
As you lift up exceptional high praises to Me, in My eyesight;
You'll excel the previous, and see the glory of God that night!

My promises will be established
While in My presence you stand;
I will reward you according to
The cleanness of your hands.
I will bring you into a large place,
For you are My delight.
I will restore what the enemy stole,
And give to you all that is right.

After coming to Me in this exceptional manner,
The glory cloud you'll see;
I will fill your human tabernacle,
Yes I will fill you with all of Me!
I'm inviting you again, to step out of the normal routine;
If you want to experience things that are rarely seen;
Giving to Me continuous praise, My glory you will see;
When exceptional praise and worship is offered unto Me!"

Reflection: I heard a message entitled *"Exceptional Praise and Worship"* based on II Chronicles 1. Solomon worshiped the Lord in an *"exceptional"* manner by offering 1,000 burnt offerings on the altar. The sweet aroma of the sacrifice ascended to God continually, resulting in everyone offering continuous praise and worship to the Lord. Solomon was then blessed to see the glory of God and was granted a wise and understanding (hearing) heart, riches, and honor. In my heart, I began to hunger to see God's glory in my own life. The Spirit of the Lord began to invite me into a new realm, to step out of the normal routine and completely into His presence where I too would be blessed to see His glory. This could only be accomplished by offering my love in an *"exceptional"* manner through continuous praise and worship. Our Lord is wonderful and is truly worthy of **"Exceptional Praise And Worship!"**

TRUE WORSHIP
THAT WHICH HE REQUIRES!

The Lord Jesus met a woman one day at a well.
Her complete life story, He began to tell.
He told her that with the water she drank, she would thirst again.
But with His living water, now her new life would begin.

Eternal life would be springing up within her today.
Our Lord began to show her, there was a much better way.
"Where do I worship, in Jerusalem or in this mount?" she said.
Jesus said, *"It will surely be different than your fathers were led".*

He began to say; *"Woman you worship you know not what, as such;*
The true worshiper is what the Father is seeking, very much".
My Lord seeks worship in spirit and in truth; this has to be rare;
To find those who will bring a heart that is truly prepared.

The hour shall come, and now it is already here,
When those who really know their God, will begin to draw near.
I tell you that the children of the Most High, will have to be inspired;
To bring true worship to the Father; giving Him that which He requires!

I have to give to my Father that which He requires me to bring.
I must give Him my praise and adoration; I must give Him everything.
Just as the clouds in the sky are formed from the vapor thereof,
My praise and worship must go up, I must send expressions of love.

For if I do not send up the vapor of my worship continually,
Where there is no vapor, there will be no rain to fall on me.
A response to my God's character is what true praise is all about.
I want to learn all about Him, so that His praise I can really shout!

My worship is my response to the wonderful relationship we share.
I'm amazed at how much He loves me; I'm so glad I know He cares.
And I will be transparent to Him, and my love will flow so free,
And the rain of His sweet Spirit, will begin to shower me!

The hour shall come, and now it is already here,
That if you really know your God, you will begin to draw near.
I tell you; that this child of the Most High, will be inspired;
To bring true worship to my Father, giving Him that which He requires!

Reflection: I visited two different churches in two different cities in the span of about a year. I marveled at the fact that I heard virtually the same message about *"true worship."* I thought, *"What are the odds of this happening?"* The second time I heard the message; the truths really began to explode in my spirit. I knew my Father was calling me to be a *"true worshiper."* In John 4, Jesus encountered the woman at the well in Samaria in order to change her life. He encounters each of us in much the same way to invite us to draw near to our Heavenly Father and respond to our love relationship with Him in *"true worship."* I found that when I send up the vapors of praise, adoration, and worship, they cause a cloud of blessing to form, which the Lord causes to rain down into my life. The elements that the *"true worshiper"* brings to the Father are spontaneity, transparency, depth and brokenness. These heart motivations and worship attitudes are mixed with the costly sacrifice of our Lord and Savior Jesus Christ. In this beautiful covenant relationship, a cloud of worship incense is produced - **"True Worship - That Which He Requires!"**

GOD'S PEACE

**"Peace I leave with you, My peace I give unto you:
not as the world giveth, give I unto you.
Let not your heart be troubled,
neither let it be afraid."
(John 14:27)**

NOT BORN TO LOSE BUT BOUND TO WIN!

There is a sad song, in the world, called *"Born to Lose"*.
But my viewpoint is different, when the Word of God, I choose.

If my God be for me, and He is on my side,
Who can be against me, when in me Jesus abides?

His own Son the Father delivered up, and did not spare,
And with Him He freely gives all things, my God really cares.

Jesus is making intercession for me at the Father's right hand.
I'm glad Christ died and rose again, for every nation and land.

Neither anything present now, nor anything that will come;
Can separate me from the love of God, in Christ Jesus the Son.

When I really began to trust in His Word, realizing that it is true,
There is nothing I can't accomplish, nothing I cannot do.

God says it in His Word, I see it again and again;
I was never born to lose, but always bound to win!

Reflection: I heard a minister say one night that ***"We are bound to win, not born to lose!"*** In the Word of God, we see that God has provided everything for victory. Jesus Christ walked the earth, led a sinless life, made the ultimate sacrifice by giving His life on the cross, and He rose again. He did it all! Christ redeemed us from the curse of the law, from poverty, sickness, and spiritual death! Truly we were **"Not Born To Lose But Bound To Win!"**

I AM YOUR SOURCE!

Yahweh Jireh is one of God's redemptive names;
I'm so glad He never changes; He's always the same.
This means my *"Provider and Source of Supply;"*
His Word tells me this - upon Him I rely.

God supplies all my needs by Christ's riches in glory;
Jesus paid the price, making it all available to me.

As I study my God's Word in Psalms, I plainly read;
Because the Lord is my Shepherd, I have everything I need.

Though Christ was rich, for my sake, He became poor,
When I think of this, how could I ask for more!

I didn't always see, Christ not only saved me from sin;
He also gave me healing and wealth, when I let Him in.

I see now He's my *"Source of Life"*, my beginning and my end.
He has given me everything, what a wonderful Friend!

I am learning to take God at His Word each day;
Now He speaks peace to my heart and I hear Him say:

"Open your spiritual eyes and you will see, of course;
You are to look only to Me dear one, I Am your Source!"

Reflection: One day I received a word from the Lord. He told me to stop looking to man to meet my needs, but look to Him. He said He wanted me to truly see Him as my Father; and that He was my *"Source."* Several months later, I received some bad financial news. At that moment the Spirit of God reminded me of that earlier word and said clearly, **"I Am Your Source!"**

A FIXED ESTABLISHED HEART

There are many things I do not understand;
There's a state of confusion on every hand.
Through my problems I question, *"Lord why me?*
I deserve better Father, can't You see?"
My Lord began to comfort me immediately;
He said, *"My Child, here is what I want you to see.*
Through life's trials, you will stand, not fall apart;
Your confession in this life is a fixed established heart!

Sure there is confusion all over this land;
But with the armor of God, you are able to stand.
My Word says that you shall not be moved forever;
I love you and will never leave you, no; not ever!
Your heart must be fixed, trusting in your Lord;
Fear, doubt, and unbelief, you cannot afford.
Through life's trials, you will stand, not fall apart;
Your confession in this life is a fixed established heart!

I know you think things do not work out, as they should.
Trust Me, I'll work these things together; for your own good.
Circumstances prevent your seeing My ability.
Please don't focus on them My Child, don't limit Me!
In your heart daily, you must plant this seed,
Look to the bigness of your Lord and not your need!
Through life's trials, you will stand, not fall apart;
Your confession in this life: 'I have a fixed established heart!'"

Reflection: I was experiencing certain problems in my life with such negative circumstances; I could not see any hope. I had a series of near devastating events happen one right after another. Physically, I was tired. I was not sleeping well and spiritually I was defeated. I began to ask, *"Why do these terrible things happen to me? What am I doing wrong?"* I went to the Word of God, to Psalm 112. This is one of my favorite Psalms because it gives a portrait of the fixed, established heart. My greatest challenge as a Christian has been to remain established despite circumstances and all that the enemy has brought against me. I began to meditate on this Psalm. The Lord spoke to my heart and told me that my confession in this life is that I have **"A Fixed, Established Heart!"**

STAND STILL AND SEE THE SALVATION OF YOUR LORD!

I love you so much Lord, but my mind is full of doubt.
There are so many things, I just cannot figure out.
I know you have the answers that I need to know.
Open up your Word to me, and please let them show.

Your Word tells me, if I would only call upon You;
You would show me things to come, and exactly what to do.
I am under pressure, to just give up and quit my Lord.
Yet I know these feelings of defeat, I cannot afford.

But when I feel like giving up, like I surely do now,
What can I do to keep from falling, please tell me how?
After having done all I know to do, You say that I'm to stand,
But my heart is slowly breaking, I don't know if I can.

My Lord said; *"Listen Child, when you gave*
Your heart, and life to Me;
One thing should have been evident,
But now you must clearly see:
That I not only saved you, and made you whole;
But your precious life is now, within My control.

Trust Me! I will make your path very clear and bright;
I will lead you in the perfect way that is right.
Now I will speak peace to your heart and mind;
They shall be in one accord.
My Word for you My Child; stand still and see
The salvation of your Lord!"

Reflection: I awoke very early one morning. I had been experiencing apparent defeat in certain areas of my life. I felt like just giving up on everything. Sometimes our lives seem like that violent storm that the disciples' thought was threatening their lives. Like them, we need to hear the voice of the Lord say to our storm *"Peace be still."* I cried out to the Lord, asking Him to please give me a word to help sustain me. As I expressed my need to the Lord, He gave me peace with His Word; **"Stand Still And See The Salvation Of Your Lord!"**

FREE TO FAIL

"You are trying too hard My Child, just let go;
I see the struggle inside that the outside doesn't show.
You are so unhappy with your failures,
And will not give them to Me;

Understand, even those things
I can transform into victory.
You want to give Me your strengths,
Your weaknesses you don't want Me to see.

But My strength is made perfect
In your weakness Child, that is the key.
Besides, what looks like failure now;
May not always be the case.

Because I see the beginning and end,
Yes, I know what you will face.
I love you so much, how do I get it across to you?
And it doesn't depend upon how well you think you do.

You can never be good enough to merit My grace;
Christ purchased this for you, so in My heart you have a place!
Please believe Me when I tell you Child, that all is well;
There will be times in life, when you must be free to fail!"

Reflection: My heart was broken. I had suffered what I perceived to be an overwhelming failure. If we love someone, we don't want to disappoint him or her. I love the Lord with all of my heart and all I could see was that I had let Him down. The Lord showed me that what I had been saying to Him was, *"Lord I failed in this situation, but I'm successful in this situation; please accept me, please love me!"* The Lord reminded me of what the enemy had blinded me from seeing. He showed me that His love for me is not dependent upon anything I do to earn it. He is *"Love"*, and I can rest in the knowledge that He sees me perfect through the precious Blood of my Lord Jesus Christ. So I stopped struggling with the concept of failure. I understand that I don't deliberately open myself to failure, but I recognize that when I do fail, the love of God in Christ Jesus is far greater than my failure. The love and mercy of God have made me **"Free To Fail!"**

A HIGHER STANDARD OF FORGIVENESS AND LOVE

My Father had a word to share with me one day.
He said; *"Child, today I will show you a better way.*
You have shadows of pain and ghosts from the past.
If you choose to release them now, the pain will not last.

I have healing balm to put your emotions together again.
Completely open your heart dear one; please let Me begin.
I will give the oil of joy, for mourning, unto you.
Putting on the garment of praise is what you must do.

Although you may not forget everything that you know;
I tell you the wounds will close, and the scars will never show.
Understand you have no future if you won't release the past.
That includes everything, release the good and the bad.

Your God is bigger than any challenge you face, that's true.
And because I live inside you, shouldn't I show through?
Listen to Me My Child, to your Father God in heaven above.
I have called you to a higher standard of forgiveness and love!"

Reflection: Many times while I'm in prayer, the Spirit of the Lord searches out and uncovers those deep-seated emotions that I may not be aware of consciously. This particular morning, God was showing me the pain and unforgiveness in my heart. Because I am a Christian and I know that God requires me to forgive others as He has forgiven me, I found that many times I would forgive with my head and not my heart. My Lord requires heart forgiveness. He does not ask me to do this in my own power or strength, but in the power of His matchless all encompassing love! Only the Spirit of the Lord can reach inside us and heal memories and soothe the pain and hurt that this life can bring over the years. Because I have experienced God's grace and forgiveness, I listened intently when He said; I have called you to **"A Higher Standard Of Forgiveness And Love!"**

I NEVER REJECTED YOU!

Lord, I marvel at man's ability to inflict pain;
It is so unnecessary and could be called insane.
We are supposed to love, not tear one another apart.
This love should begin, when we ask Christ into our heart.
Unfortunately, there are those who name Christ's name,
But a change never takes place; they are exactly the same.

They harshly judge others, and do not show God's love;
It's hard to believe, they could be born from above.
Christ came not into the world to condemn it for sin;
He came to save the world that we might be born again!
It's sad that my mistakes, others would not forget;
I'm so glad God forgot, when the Lord Jesus I met!

And over the years, some have hurt and rejected me;
But through all of this, my Father's grace I was to see.
From the beginning, it seems I have heard my Lord say;
And I keep this close to my heart each and every day.
"This world can be cruel and insensitive, that is true;
Please remember My Child, I never rejected you!"

Reflection: One day God gave me a word. He said; *"In the past, you have done My will and others have rejected you for it, but Cindy I never rejected you!"* Rejection hurts, but as Christians we know Christ was rejected and we will be too. Jesus was not always understood and He let us know that we will be misunderstood also. I believe we expect rejection from the world, but when it happens within the Body of Christ, the pain is deeper. I was talking to someone who had faced rejection from a church body and I could see the pain in her heart. I told her that Christ never rejected her! When I said that, I remembered God's word to me and I began to write; **"I Never Rejected You!"** Because truly, God says that He will always love and be there for us, even when people let us down.

THE GOD SITUATION!

Sometimes in the natural realm, things do not look good;
We become convinced things are not working, as they should.
We look at the world situation in the evening news;
And become alarmed, confused, and yes, even fearful too.
The finances of this world are in a collapsed state;
Wall Street reports daily, and for this the world waits.

It is obvious this situation looks very grave indeed;
But I will cling to the Word of God to meet my every need.
God says in the natural not to be moved by what I see;
And in the spiritual, I see no shortage, in His economy!
My Father is rich; He owns everything there is;
The earth and all its fullness, I know are plainly His.

This situation with shortage and lack, I will not face.
God promised to supply my need through His abundant grace.
I may be in a battle, but I know I don't have to wait.
Now is the time to praise, and begin to celebrate.
I won't regard the world situation; praise God, now I will shout;
Because I know what the *"God Situation"* is really all about!

Reflection: One day our Christian group was discussing things we wanted to accomplish in the Lord. The question was asked; *"What is the money situation like?"* One of my friends asked; *"What is the 'God situation' like?"* As that phrase hit my spirit, I thought, *"That is the question that always should be asked"*. We must learn to trust in the Lord's abundant supply, not merely our own. There certainly is an abundant supply in Christ, so I decided to explore **"The God Situation!"**

HOW MUCH I HAVE GROWN!

If I am moved by what I feel, or what I see;
Then my Lord cannot accomplish what He would in me.
I am not like a wave of the sea, driven and tossed.
I am secure in my Jesus, not confused or lost.

Double minded and unstable in my ways, I will not be.
Letting patience have her perfect work, that is the key.
Though many troubles in this life, I have faced,
Yet I have survived and grown, through my God's grace.

But during times of trial and testing,
Discouragement I had found.
I began to cry to the Lord,
"My God I'm losing ground!"

He said; *"You must offer to Me the sacrifice of praise;*
And give Me thanksgiving, and the name of Jesus raise.
The tears the enemy has caused you to shed in the night;
Believe Me, I will turn it around, and I'll make it all right.

You see, for in joy you shall reap,
For in tears you have sown;
And I am glad to say dear Child,
I have seen how much you've grown!"

Reflection: In my walk with the Lord, there have been times that I felt that I had ceased to grow or that I was going backwards because of so many trials in my life. I began to say to the Lord that I had not pleased Him. I also said I should just give up because I was not facing the trials the way He wanted. As I expressed these feelings to the Lord, He answered and showed me just **"How Much I Have Grown!"**

I KNOW THE THOUGHTS I HAVE TOWARD YOU!

At this point in your life, you are wondering what to do.
But your God says; *"Child I know the thoughts I have toward you!*

*They are good thoughts and plans for welfare and peace.
The confusion you feel now will surely cease.*

*You think, 'I don't understand the plan; it must be wrong!'
I am asking you to trust Me and just purpose to be strong.*

*I'm saying to you; do not be weary in doing well.
You will reap if you don't allow a fainting spell.*

*I know the fulfillment of My plans for you; you want to see.
I'll guide you one step at a time because the end is really Me!*

*My plans for you are not evil; in your life My will be done.
To give you an expected end, yes hope in your final outcome!*

*At this point in your life, you are wondering what to do.
But remember My Child; I know the thoughts I have toward you!"*

Reflection: I was standing at the crossroads of life. I had a decision to make that was to affect my entire future. I was wondering what my life would be like and what the Lord had in store for me. The Spirit of the Lord quickened to my heart, Jeremiah 29:11; where He is speaking to the nation of Israel. They were in captivity in Babylon and God promised to visit them and release them. He assured them that His thoughts toward them were good thoughts to strengthen and give them hope. It seemed that for several days I was hearing this scripture in my spirit. My Father began to speak to my heart and say; **"I Know The Thoughts I Have Toward You!"**

GOD'S PURPOSE

"There are many devices in a man's heart; nevertheless the counsel of the LORD, that shall stand." (Proverbs 19:21)

IF NOT YOU - WHO?
IF NOT NOW - WHEN?

My Heavenly Father asked me today,
As I went along my own merry way.
And I heard Him ask it again and again:
"If not you - who? If not now - when?"

I began to meditate upon what He meant.
But my day was so busy and off I went.
Forgetting that thought He had placed within:
"If not you - who? If not now - when?"

The Spirit of God again reminded me.
This time I asked, *"Lord please help me to see."*
He asked, *"Is the love of God in your heart?*
That's where you begin, yes, that's where you start.

The harvest is plenteous, the laborers few.
Enter the harvest field now; I surely need you.
There's a world of lost people dying in sin.
If not you - who? If not now - when?

Now is not the time to be slothful or slack.
Soon the Lord Jesus Christ will be coming back.
The world has to know My Son freed them from sin.
For you there's a harvest to reap, yes souls to win!

Sharing the wonderful good news, that's the key.
Tell Me, 'Here am I Lord, I'm ready, send me.
To tell of Christ's wondrous love, time and again!'
My Child: if not you - who? And if not now - when?"

Reflection: I attended a secular meeting one night. The speaker's theme was on social reform and changing our society through greater awareness and education. The title of his message was ***"If Not You - Who? If Not Now - When?"*** The following week, the Spirit of God kept giving me that phrase. Social reform is fine, but what the world needs now is Jesus! Society cannot make a significant change unless men and women's hearts are changed by the miracle of the new birth in Christ Jesus. My Heavenly Father asked me **"If Not You - Who? If Not Now - When?"**

I'LL GIVE ALL OF MY LIFE TO YOU!

One day while praying, the Lord began to speak to my heart:
"I have a word of wisdom for you, knowledge to impart.
Confessing with your mouth, that Jesus is Lord,
Having both your heart and mouth in one accord.
Believing in your heart, from the dead, Jesus was raised,
And confessing this with your mouth, is how you were saved!
This is the way it all began for you; this was your start.
You were born again that day, as you asked Me into your heart.
You know many people accept Me as Savior of their soul;
But not as Lord of their life, they want ultimate control.

They want Me to take them to heaven when they die;
But totally giving Me their life, they will not comply.
Don't be like the others; they are in danger of a big fall.
Because if I'm not Lord of their lives, then I'm not Lord at all.
When I ask you to do something, don't say, 'Lord, no'.
If I am really your Lord, then that word has to go.
Am I really the center of your life?
Or have you left your first love?
Have you stopped trusting in the
Power of your God in heaven above?

I know you love Me and have committed your life to Me;
But what I want from you is surrender, unconditionally.
I tell you this because I love you,
I must be Savior and Lord.
To live your life any other way dear one,
You just cannot afford.
Precious Child, today I will tell you
What I am prepared to do;
If you'll give all of your life to Me,
I'll give all of My life to you!"

Reflection: I had reached a point in my life where to follow the path the Lord was telling me to walk was causing me much pain. We, as human beings, tend to want to take the easier, and what seems to us, the less complicated road. But God, who sees the beginning from the end, is asking us to trust. While His way may seem painful for a while, it will end with glorious triumph! *"Unconditional Surrender"* was the word the Lord had for me this day. So I surrendered my will to give Him the Lordship of my life and I accepted His promise when He said, **"I'll Give All Of My Life To You!"**

THE LORD OF THE HARVEST

The Lord of the harvest is speaking to my heart right now.
He says, *"I want to get this truth across, someway, somehow.
You say that you understand that these are the last days.
But I do not see this reflected in all of your ways.*

*The cares of this world have choked the Word in you.
It has happened not only to you, but others too!
Do you really understand, that many will be lost;
If you and others are not willing to bear the cost?*

*The fields are already white to harvest, Child lift up your eyes.
They are asking for deliverance, can't you hear their cries?
Now is not the time for you, to sit down and take your rest.
It is the time to reap; says the Lord of the harvest!*

*'I just cannot reach them all!' I hear you say;
But I say, that is why you must be faithful to pray.
The harvest is plentiful, and the laborers are few;
Pray the Lord of the harvest, to do what you cannot do!*

*And into His harvest, He will send laborers to meet,
And make those who will receive Him, whole and complete.
There are eternal wages for sowers and reapers to receive;
Do not let the enemy distract you; I say, do not be deceived!*

*Listen to My Word; take heed, and hear My voice;
Because in My Kingdom, those who sow and reap rejoice!
So now is not the time for you, to sit down and take your rest.
It is the time to reap; says the Lord of the harvest!"*

Reflection: In Matt. 9:37, Jesus states, *"The harvest is truly plenteous, but the laborers are few".* I was to give a message, and the theme of the program was Matt. 9:37-38. The Lord began to confirm my message with this poem. My mind went back several years to an experience that I had forgotten. I had shared the gospel with a high school friend, and at that point in his life, he was not receptive. He was filled with bitterness. I wondered if I had missed God by even trying to share with him at all. The Spirit of the Lord showed me that I was in His will at that time. He then showed me other people that I personally knew who were lost. I cried, *"Lord God I can't reach them all!"* He simply wanted me to wake up and have enough love and compassion in my heart to pray for them. He wanted me to pray for **"The Lord Of The Harvest"** to send the perfect laborers into His harvest, that others might receive Him.

PRECIOUS SEED!

In myself there is nothing special, this I understand.
The same could be said, about every woman and man.
Yet I marvel that the Father chose me to receive His love,
He sent it in the form of His only Son from heaven above.
I received Jesus; the Word of God, He is my *"Precious Seed"*.
He loved me enough to die for me, and set me free indeed!

My Lord said, *"You are special, because I now live inside of you;*
And others need to know they are just as important to Me too.
Go forth with weeping, taking precious seed to bear.
There are many that are lost, tell Me, do you really care?
After bearing precious seed, you shall doubtless come again,
Bringing your sheaves with you, with even more souls to win!"

So I am glad to bear the message of love untold,
Telling those that I meet, who are lost and cold.
Jesus died and was raised again, to meet your every need,
If you receive my Lord and Love, He'll be your *"Precious Seed!"*

Reflection: I know that without Christ, I am nothing and can do nothing. With Christ, I am special and can do all things! I'm so glad to belong to Jesus and my greatest joy is for others to receive Him and all that He offers. Psalms 126 states; they that sow in tears shall reap in joy. One of the most fulfilling things in life is sowing the seed of the love of God in someone's heart and watching the harvest. Jesus is the manifestation of the Father's love for us and He can be called a **"Precious Seed!"**

WHO IS MY MOTHER OR BRETHREN?

One day the Lord's mother and brethren were standing about;
Wishing to speak to Him, they sent a message to call Him out.
They not only stood without; but had no desire to come in;
But they tried to interrupt those, receiving the Word within.
But Jesus was intent upon His work, seed had to be sown;
He came to do the Father's will, not seeking to do His own.

Who is my mother or my brethren? Jesus is asking you.
It is those who not only hear the Word, but are doers of it too!

As for me, I have His nature and image; I even bear His name;
His love has completely changed me, I have never been the same!
Others are to see the Word of God, perfected in me,
As I strive to reflect the love of Jesus, for all the world to see.
I look upon every Christian, who seeks to do the Lord's will,
As the Lord's brother, sister, mother, the Word of God to fulfill.

Who is my mother or my brethren? Jesus is asking you.
It is those who not only hear the Word, but are doers of it too!

Reflection: The Lord had given me a word concerning a message I was to give. I began to meditate on the scripture references He had given me. Jesus said; *"My mother and my brethren are these which hear the word of God and do it"* (Luke 8:21). Jesus owns as His nearest and most precious relations those who hear the Word of God and do it! So the Lord is asking, **"Who Is My Mother Or Brethren?"**

MY FATHER KNOWS BEST

I was making wrong decisions in my life;
They were causing me pain, sorrow, and strife.
I wondered, *"How can I change this pattern of sorrow;*
Affecting not only today, but also my tomorrow?"

Jesus said, *"I Am the Good Shepherd, My voice you know;*
And the voice of a stranger, you will not follow.
Other voices are loud, causing confusion and rush.
God speaks in a still small voice, with a sense of hush.
Stop listening to those other voices from outside.
Listen to the Spirit's voice, in you He abides.
Proving that good and perfect will of God, you will find,
By being transformed, by the renewing of your mind.
With the living Word of God your mind is renewed;
You daily feed your body; your spirit too needs food!
Then in the Lord, put your trust, and commit your way.
And you will have peace with your decisions each day".

So I committed my way to my All Knowing Friend;
Realizing my God knows the beginning from the end.
There are many voices in this life; I won't listen to the rest.
I have full assurance in my heart, my Father knows best!

Reflection: I find that there are a variety of ways that I write my poetry. Sometimes hearing or reading a phrase or title, or meditating on a specific concern in my heart; will cause me to write a poem. One day I was reading the TV Guide and came across the old TV show, *"Father Knows Best".* I thought to myself; *"What a good title for a poem!"* My Heavenly Father does know best! I began to think about how each decision we make affects our lives in some way. I thought about how the Bible tells us how to tap into God's wisdom and knowledge to make the right decisions in life. So I began to express my desire to the Lord to make right decisions with His help because **"My Father Knows Best!"**

GOD'S PLAN

"I have glorified thee on the earth: I have finished the work which thou gavest me to do."
(John 17:4)

CHOOSE WHO YOU WILL SERVE TODAY!

There is a decision to be made in my life each day;
As I rise each morning, I could choose either way.
I could choose the way of the world and be like the rest;
Or I could choose my Father's way, which I know is best.

He said; *"I call heaven and earth to record this day against you;*
I set before you blessing and cursing; also life and death too.
Therefore choose life today that you may live;
There is so much for you to do, so much to give.

So choose My Child, who you will serve today;
Remember, he who does My work will get My pay!
I Am the Lord your God that you may love;
I Am the God of all the earth and the heaven above.

Obey My voice, cleave unto Me, I Am the length of your days;
I Am your life dear one, I will bless you in so many ways.
I would like everything with you, to be well;
And in the land I promised, I want you to dwell.

Therefore choose life today that you may live.
There is so much for you to do, so much to give.
So choose My Child, who you will serve today;
Remember, he who does My work will get My pay!"

Reflection: I was reading Deut. 30:19, when the Spirit of the Lord began to deal with me. The choice is set before us by the Lord and that choice is *"life or death"* and *"blessing or curse"*. The Spirit of the Lord impressed me that in my life, this would not simply be a one-time choice, but a choice for *"life and blessing"* that I must consciously make every day of my life. He showed me that true *"life and blessing"* is in Him alone and He will reward. The rewards that the world offers cannot compare to the blessings of the Lord. Proverbs 10:22 states; His blessings make us rich and no sorrow added with it. In effect, the Spirit of the Lord desires a choice each day. He is saying; **"Choose Who You Will Serve Today!"**

SLEEPING DAUGHTER: ARISE AND AWAKE!

I know that in my life right now, a change it's time to make;
I hear the Holy Spirit say, *"Sleeping daughter, arise and awake!*
It is the season to go from here, to another place;"
He is calling me away to Him, an encounter face-to-face.
I am not to remember the past, or consider the things of old.
I'm called to a future of purpose, with direction bright and bold.
Springing forth will be a new thing, which I had no vision to see;
But I believe with all my heart, His glory will be revealed to me.

For so long I have felt in my life I have been slumbering or asleep;
It's the type of rest without benefit; my purpose, unable to keep.
And it's easy to settle down now, not considering what's at stake;
Realizing what the cost could be, I keep hearing the word *"Awake".*
And I hear the Spirit say; *"Arise and you will go from here;*
Do not give place to doubt, I say you are not to fear.
New things, new things, will come forth springing;"
And the joy His Word brings, is in my heart ringing!

And in the wilderness His angels prepare a road just for me;
And the precious Spirit will flow, His River will set me free.
I want so much for my Heavenly Father
To finish in me the work He has begun;
For He has created in me the wonderful desire
To be conformed to His dear Son.
There has been a war raging in my spirit;
But God knows I want what's right.

Just now I sense the Spirit of Grace
Leading me from darkness into light.
Yes, I know that in my life right now,
A change it's time to make;
I hear the Holy Spirit say again,
"Sleeping daughter, arise and awake!"

Reflection: I had known for a few months that my life was in the midst of a major change. I had made some right decisions that year relative to my calling and purpose in God's plan. There were more decisions to make. I was apprehensive about the change and the resulting future and wanted to pull back. But I could not miss the idea that the Spirit of the Lord was calling me away to Him, to a face-to-face encounter, relative to areas of incompleteness in my life. He wanted to make the needed changes in my life and His call to me was; **"Sleeping Daughter, Arise And Awake!"**

ASK ME LORD PLEASE; I WANT TO SAY YES!

Too many things in life, my Lord I fail to see.
But my confession has to be, that I trust in Thee.
Dwelling in the Secret Place, and under Your shadow;
You will forever be my fortress Lord, this I know.

Like a bird finding shelter, under Your wing;
I know that in You, I am safe from everything.
Your truth will be my buckler, and my shield;
Lord, You have my heart, to You I must yield.

I know I must trust in You, for my prayer to come true.
To do every task, You have called me to do.
Because I want my life to be one that will bless;
Ask me Lord please; I want to say yes!

I'm not afraid of the arrow by day, nor the terror by night.
Please Jesus direct my path, in the way that is right.
Lord, You're my refuge, my habitation, my Most High.
I must learn to trust in You, without the need to ask why.

I trust You to perfect everything, concerning me;
Especially those things my own eyes don't readily see.
I know I must trust in You, as my help in time of trouble;
Or unbelief will drown my spirit, and my life will be a struggle.

My God above all, I want to make sure I hear Your voice;
So in Your presence, I will have reason to rejoice.
Because I want my life to be one that will bless;
Ask me Lord please; I want to say yes!

Reflection: It is so easy to say that you trust in the Lord when everything is going your way. But when things are not going your way, do you still trust in the Lord? I found that I did not. I was hurt and confused and so many things were happening to me that I just could not understand. But through my confusion, I declared; *"Lord I trust You."* I was reading Psalms 91 and I began to see that trusting in the Lord is the key; trusting in His goodness and His love no matter what life brings our way. Because I was hurting, I had been ready to say *"no"* to everything. But in my spirit I cried; **"Ask Me Lord Please; I Want To Say Yes!"**

I WANT TO BE YOUR SUPERSTAR!

Once upon a time, in sin, I was lost;
Not realizing Someone had paid the cost.
The gospel of Jesus Christ was told to me;
I saw the Light, thank God now I'm free!
I found I could make a brand new start;
If I would only ask Him into my heart.
I asked, *"Lord Jesus, please come in;*
And cleanse me from my burden of sin."
He heard my prayer and He saved my soul;
He's so good; I was completely made whole!
I accepted the Lord, and it was only the start;
Now there's another prayer that is on my heart.
I want to be fully aware of Christ's identity;
I know the Spirit of the Lord will reveal Him to me.
Lord, I want to see You as You really are;
Then Lord, I can become Your superstar!

Lord, I don't care if the world knows my name;
I could care less about worldly fortune or fame.
I want to enter in, so that Your voice I will hear;
So that I will be able to speak Your message clear.
But I do want heaven to know my name;
I want them to say, *"She boldly proclaims!"*
And for Jesus to say, *"Father, she confesses before men;*
About the gift of God and cleansing from sin."
I want to know You Lord, in resurrection power;
And set free the captive, every minute, every hour.
These things I want, for Your praise and Your glory;
When time ends, eternity will tell the story.
When I see You Jesus, I want to know I've done my best;
I want to hear You say, *"Well done, enter into My rest."*
Lord, I have to see You as You really are;
Only then Lord, can I become Your superstar!

Reflection: Some time ago, the Lord showed me that there is a great Christian identity crisis. Many Christians don't really know Who Jesus Christ is and who they are in Him. Having revelation knowledge of these truths will totally transform the life of the believer. Oh, how I wanted this change for my life! I said to a Christian friend one day that it just wasn't worth it to me to just live my life as an average Christian. I told him that I wanted to be a superstar in the Lord. I don't want to be the world's idea of a superstar, but God's idea of one; knowing the reality of Who Christ is and who I am in Him. A few weeks later, I began to tell the Lord**, "I Want To Be Your Superstar!"**

I MUST ENTER IN!

The Lord Jesus Christ is my changeless High Priest;
His Priesthood is perfect, never to cease.
He's on the right hand of the throne of Majesty;
Ever living to make intercession for me.

The Blood of Jesus Christ paid the price for sin;
That into God's throne room I might enter in.
I can boldly come to the throne of grace;
It's wonderful to know He purchased my place!

Until now I've only come part of the way through;
There's a cry in my spirit, and I know what to do.
Lord, I only know one way to begin;
I want to, I need to, I must enter in!

My Lord is telling me: *"Go beyond the veil;*
I will meet with you there My Child, all is well.
There are things I want to tell you, things to share;
Of wondrous secrets, I want to make you aware.

With the things I tell you, souls you will reach;
Think of all of those I have given you to teach.
Remember, I have chosen you, you have not chosen Me;
My heart is set upon you, for My praise and My glory.

You will bring forth fruit; it will be much;
Good fruit, eternal, that others see and touch.
Yes, there's only one way for you to begin;
You want to, you need to, you must enter in!"

Now I'm with my Eternal High Priest in the heavens above;
In Your presence, I clearly see You, my Lord of Love.
As I draw nigh unto You, You will draw nigh unto me;
In Your presence is fullness of peace and prosperity.

At Your right hand there are pleasures forever more;
With fullness of love, joy, and direction in store.
Basking in Your love, I have rest in my soul;
Only in Your presence am I completely made whole.

What this world has, I don't need to get through;
Everything that I need Lord, I found in You.
Lord, I only know one way to begin;
I want to, I need to, and praise God, I have entered in!

Reflection: The Lord revealed to me that most of my frustration in life stemmed from the fact that I had never really entered into His presence. Oh, there were times that I had to some degree, but I was not consistent. The week I wrote this poem, I kept saying over and over to the Lord; *"I need to, I want to, I must enter in."* I remembered earlier invitations by the Spirit of God not to spend time in the Inner Court, but go directly into the presence of God because in Him, all fullness dwells. He began to show me that absolutely everything that I need in this life can be found in His presence. **"I Must Enter In"** in order to hear the Lord's voice and become what He would have me to be! At the end of that week, I received a word from the Lord telling me that He had heard the cry in my spirit and was prepared to give me new direction and confirm His will in my life.

THE CHURCH WITHOUT WALLS

One night while in prayer, I heard my Lord say;
*"I will speak to you My Child, in My own sweet, gentle way.
Arise and shine, for your light has come;
Arise from your sleep and take your place in the Son.
I have called you to be a reflector of light;
With the glory of the Lord, shining ever so bright.*

*I will build My Church, it will be without wrinkle or spot;
A glorious Church is My desire, that which I have sought.
To be radiant and bright, bringing glorious deliverance;
Not held back in darkness, from depression and circumstance!
Nations coming to the brightness of your light, I want you to see;
As you let your light shine before them, they will be drawn to Me!*

*My Spirit will be upon you, with righteousness and glory;
To grant unto those that mourn, comfort and joy to set them free.
So arise and shine, for your light has come;
Arise from your sleep and take your place in the Son.
You see, I Am building My Church in you, so hear My call;
Understand, you shall be called, 'The Church Without Walls!' "*

Reflection: It seemed like a very long time since I had experienced the intimacy I once knew in my relationship with the Lord. It is so sad when we allow the cares, disappointments, and trials of this life to rob us and separate us from the One Who is anointed to take care of our burdens. But the Lord is so loving and so faithful that He draws us back to Himself with cords of love. I was talking to a minister friend of mine this particular night. He, not so gently, rebuked me for my careless attitude concerning the call God had placed on my life. He shared many impressions from the Lord. The Holy Spirit confirmed in my heart the things that he shared. After hanging up the phone, I began to pray and was led to read Isaiah 60. As I was reading, the Spirit of the Lord began to speak to my heart. I could see that Isaiah 60 is a chapter of prophetic promises of restoration to Israel. But the Lord also showed me the Messianic message and how believers are to allow Christ to live His life through them. We are to let our light shine before men that they may see our good works that bring glory to our Heavenly Father. The *"Light"* of Christ in us will draw those in need of deliverance. Because this *"Light"* lives in me, the Lord said, *"You shall be called* **'The Church Without Walls!'"**

I WANT TO SAY "I HAVE FINISHED MY WORK!"

Father, as I read Your Word, there's something on my heart;
I know Your precious Spirit is here, with knowledge to impart.
Jesus said; *"I have finished the work You have given Me to do;"*
Through the life He lived on this earth, He glorified You.
He went about seeking to do Your will, listening to Your voice;
Knowing when His work was done, He would be able to rejoice.
To show mankind all about Your love, for this cause Jesus came;
And His heart's desire above all else, was to glorify Your name.

Before the foundations of the world,
You knew Your child I would be;
You purposed in Your heart and mind,
That You would make me free.
Lord, I know there are tasks,
That You have given each of us to do;
And I know my talents become gifts,
Only as they are touched by You.

My Lord said: *"I've cleared your path*
Of all barriers, and have made you free;
Each and every day you will make a choice,
Please choose to glorify Me.
From your mother's womb, there are works
That I have called you to do;
And take note My Child,
They are designed especially for you!"

Lord, hear the heart cry of my spirit; I want to be able to say;
When I come and stand before You, in heaven on that day:
"My Father, on the earth through my life I have glorified You;
Because I have finished the work, You have given me to do!"

Reflection: I was reading John 17:4, where Jesus said, *"I have glorified thee on earth: I have finished the work which thou gavest me to do."* I thought, what an awesome statement for my Lord to make. Jesus was our great example of how to submit our lives in love to the Father's plan and purpose. I began to reflect upon the truth in Ephesians 1:4; that He had chosen me before the foundation of the world to glorify His name. We live our lives so much of the time as if God has no purpose, plan, or design for us. He indeed does have a plan for every human being and the choice is ours as to whether we will take the time to find and fulfill it. The day I wrote these words, I envisioned myself standing before Him in heaven someday. In my heart, I began to tell my Heavenly Father; **"I Want To Say I Have Finished My Work!"**

GOD'S "PERSONAL" LOVE

"The LORD hath appeared of old unto me, saying, 'Yea, I have loved thee with an everlasting love: therefore with lovingkindness have I drawn thee.'"
(Jeremiah 31:3)

A LETTER FROM JESUS - (TO JEAN)

"I love you; you're a flower Jean;
Lovely, fragrant, and one rarely seen.
I have looked inside; you are pure in heart;
And I knew that, from the very start.

Your spirit is gentle and very meek,
In character you cannot be called weak.
I have chosen you, to shout forth my praise,
I have prepared you for that, in so many ways.

For many good works, have I fashioned thee,
Eternity will tell, you just wait and see.
And on that day when you look upon My face;
You will know, above all, you have run a good race.

With all of your heart and soul, continue to seek Me;
And a marvelous and glorious portion
Will be yours in victory.
I love you; you're a flower Jean;
Lovely, fragrant, and one rarely seen!"

Reflection: My sister-in-law, Jean, is a very special person. She is also my sister in Christ. I admire her greatly and am blessed by the beautiful gifts God has given her. She asked me to write a poem for her. At that time, I did not take my gift seriously, and didn't really regard her request. Several months later, after being in prayer one evening, to my surprise, in my spirit, I heard the Lord say these words to Jean. So I entitled it, **"A Letter From Jesus - To Jean."** After sharing it with her, she told me that the Holy Spirit had just recently spoken to her heart the very same things!

MY MOTHER'S LOVE

Mom, I don't often stop to tell you,
Just how I really feel.
But, it's burning in my heart right now;
My love for you, that's very real.
When I think of your love Mom,
I think of my Savior's great love.
Because you gave me natural birth,
And Jesus gave me birth from above.

I have stopped to reflect upon all
The things you have done for me.
God gave you the capacity to be so sweet,
Yes, it's He who holds the key.
It's not the big things Mom,
But the little things you do.
And it makes you special beyond compare;
Nothing could be more true!
Mom, I'm so grateful for the years
The Lord has blessed us to share.
And I thank Him ever so much
For a mother that took the time to care.

Mom, I want to be with you throughout
The endless ages of eternity.
And I'm believing God with all I have,
That you will be with me.
When I began to really look at you,
I knew there had to be a God above.
Because there is absolutely nothing so precious
As my mother's love!

Reflection: Another Mother's Day was approaching. I began to think of how very special my mother really is. Anyone who meets her cannot deny that she is truly a unique woman. I have always admired her capacity to love and to give of herself. This Mother's Day, I wanted to somehow tell her how much she meant to me. I knew that a store bought greeting card could not say what I wanted to say. But I knew that the Spirit of God could help me tell her. Proverbs 31:28 says; *"Her children arise up, and call her blessed."* This poem is dedicated to the most blessed and wonderful mother in the world because there is nothing so precious as **"My Mother's Love!"**

MY FATHER'S LOVE

Dad, what's in my heart and mind,
I don't really have the words to say.
I only know I need to express my love,
In some small, yet special way.
I thank my God for the strong
Father figure that you are.
Your love, guidance, and patience
Have sustained me thus far.

You gave me the will to succeed,
And in everything excel.
You taught me not to just be average,
But try and do things well.
Sometimes when you look at me,
I know it's difficult to believe and see;
That now I am all grown up,
But Dad, your little girl I'll always be.
I don't know why the Lord blessed me,
With a father like you.
I pray that you feel blessed,
To have me for a daughter too.

There is one thing though I'm sure of,
And without a doubt I know;
The wonderful lesson my Heavenly Father
Has attempted to show.
That the love of you my earthly father,
Is simply meant to reflect;
The great love my Heavenly Father has for me,
And its profound effect!

Reflection: I had written a poem for my mother for Mother's Day. I knew I needed to tell my dad how much I loved and appreciated him too. So I wrote a Father's Day poem for him. My dad is such a wonderful man. I thought of how fortunate I was to have such a good relationship with my father. When I received Jesus Christ as my Lord and Savior, it was so easy to see God as my Father because of the great pattern of love and care that my earthly father had given me. This poem is dedicated to the most wonderful father in the world! I am blessed to see **"My Father's Love"** in both my earthly father and my Heavenly Father!

MY ANOINTING WILL HEAL YOUR BROKEN HEART!

Father, my heart is hurt; I ask do You really care?
There is pain inside my heart, and there's nothing to compare.
All my life, my emotions, have been battered and abused;
The endless hurt keeps growing; I'm so tired, and yes, confused.

A root of bitterness is growing up, on the inside of me;
Father my heart is crying to You, I need Your help, can't You see?
I've been rejected so much, I find it hard to trust in anyone's love;
Please Lord; don't let me lose sight
Of Your perfect gifts, from heaven above.

I heard my Lord say, *"Don't let the pain and hurt, tear you apart;*
Remember it is My anointing, that will heal your broken heart.
My Child, I never rejected you; that is for sure;
But for the terrible hurt, I have the perfect cure.
I know others have been cruel, and they have treated you cold;
Remember not the former things, nor consider the things of old.
Before I can do a new thing in your life, I want you to see;
All the unforgiveness must go, please give it to Me!

I will remind you of this, for you Christ died on Calvary;
He bore your pain and sorrow,
And His precious love will set you free.
Instead of letting the pain and hurt, tear you apart;
Please remember, it is My anointing
That will heal your broken heart!"

Reflection: I saw a friend of mine one night. It was very obvious that she was in a lot of emotional pain. I tried to comfort her that night, but nothing seemed to help. I had read a new poem that night and the last thing she said to me was to write a poem for her. The next morning, I woke up and thought of her and began to pray. Suddenly, I found that I could really feel her pain and I began to write her cry to the Lord and His answer to her. Human beings may reject or hurt us, but God never does. We can always depend upon His love and also His power to heal all those hurts. God said to her, **"My Anointing Will Heal Your Broken Heart!"**

A LETTER FROM JESUS "I WAITED PATIENTLY IN LINE"

*"I watched carefully inside your mother, as you were formed.
As I continued to watch you grow, my heart was warmed.
I was there and I saw you, as you began to walk.
Would you believe that I was there, as you began to talk?
I was with you when at school you entered your first class.
Can't you see I was there in every part of your past?
I was there as you went along in school, those first seven years.
I comforted every fear and wiped away all of your tears.
Then off to Junior High School you promptly went.
Did you know that with you, My Angel I sent?*

*And High School was really a milestone to complete.
Guess Who was there and had a ringside seat?
Then off you went to college, embarking on life's journey.
I didn't even leave you then; Oh I pray that you could see!
I was there sealing your commitment, to the one you love.
You know love is that perfect gift; I give from heaven above.
I was there ensuring the safety, of you and your little one.
That precious little baby boy, your pride and joy; your son.*

*Looking down through the years, you will see,
I was there all the way through.
You see I love you with a passion;
Nothing could be more true.
These many years I have wanted your love;
And to live inside your heart.
And throughout all the endless ages;
We would never have to part.
But I will have to wait until you want Me;
As I want you; that is fine.
Someday you will realize I was always there;
Waiting patiently in line."*

Reflection: A very dear friend of mine had never asked Jesus to come into her heart. She had gone to church for years, not realizing that it's not *"religion"* you need but a *"relationship"* with Jesus Christ, the Son of the Living God. She was experiencing difficult times in her life. I shared my faith with her and she asked me to write a poem for her. I asked the Lord what He wanted to say to her. The Spirit of God reminded me that when I received Christ, I immediately felt the reality of His presence. However, the fact remained that He was there all of the time, waiting patiently. This poem was written for my friend and can only be described as **"A Letter From Jesus - I Waited Patiently In Line."** Incidentally, after sharing this poem with her, my friend asked Jesus to become Lord and Savior of her life! Praise God!

TRUST ME!

"To begin with, I must ask you, What is trust?
It is hope and faith in Me, an absolute must!

Believe Me, I know the burdens that you bear;
Let Me help you, these burdens I'm willing to share.
When you hurt, I hurt too, you're a part of Me;
I want to share everything with you, can't you see?
You know when I came to earth and lived as a man;
I overcame this world, so with Me, you also can.
I felt love, joy, and pain, these emotions that are so real;
I experienced them to help you, to identify with what you feel.
Amidst all of your problems, your stress and your strife;
Trust that I, your Lord, have a plan for your life.

In your human thoughts you question,
'How wrong must be the plan?'
But on that day when you see My face,
You will fully understand.
On that day you'll perceive your lifetime
As having traveled many miles;
And you will also see I walked beside you,
Throughout all of the trials.

You must realize, I've made you My child
To have you share in My glory;
Soon the realm of time will end,
And eternity will tell the story.
Remember, the things you cannot understand now,
Just keep looking above.
And please rely on My goodness,
And most important of all, My love.

To end with, I must ask you, What is trust?
It is hope and faith in Me, an absolute must!"

Reflection: It's exciting to be a Christian! You never know whom the Lord may bring across your path. I met a dear woman one night in a restaurant while I was on a business trip. She was a new convert and had many problems in her life that she felt free to share with me. I spent several hours with her and I shared some of my poetry. She asked if the Lord should have a word for her, to please mail it to her. When I got home, I asked the Lord what He wanted to say to her through me. His reply was **"Trust Me!"**

I AM THE POTTER

"I Am the Potter, you are the clay.
I'll make you over, make you over today.
I see pain and rejection in that heart.
Pain is not just an end, but a brand new start.

Dear one, I see the confusion, problems, and strife.
Through My Word, you're an overcomer in this life.
I have looked inside, there is so much doubt.
That has to go, let Me just take it out.

There is also unbelief; to Me that's a crime.
That does not belong in you at any time.
I have seen your heart, when unwilling to give.
And I've seen a heart learning truly how to live.

There seems to be a recurring question of love.
Remember, I'm with you always; I'm the Heavenly Dove.
I see room inside for my glorious power.
It's available to you, every minute and hour.

These are changes you must allow Me to make.
I love you; it's only for your own sake.
I'm happy with the outcome, and with what I see.
What I'm really looking for is a reflection of Me!
You see I Am the Potter, you are the clay.
I have made you over, made you over today!"

Reflection: I met a very special lady with a tremendously sweet spirit. She was experiencing the devastation of having her marriage end. But I admired the strength she showed and I also noted *"The Source"* of her strength. There was such growth in her life in a very short period of time. The Lord gave me this poem for her one morning. When I shared it with her, she confirmed the word by telling me that she had been praying for God to have His own way in her life. He answered her by saying **"I Am The Potter!"**

THE BEST IS YET TO COME!

"As you reflect upon your life, I want you to see;
That many good works, I have before ordained for thee.
You were fashioned for these works, once you let Me in;
As God's workmanship in Christ, made to walk in them.
As under-shepherd to Jesus, you faithfully pastor your flock;
And have given your life to feed them,
The mysteries of God to unlock.
In your home you are functioning,
As God's high priest of your family;
With the patience of Christ as Head,
Yes, His love being the ultimate key!

You have brought the message of hope,
And good news on your radio show;
As you have sought to glorify your Father,
The blessings of heaven will flow.
Yes, My blessings upon your life,
Have been great in measure;
But I want to tell you this,
And it brings Me much pleasure:
Because your life is hid with Christ in God,
Please receive this truth My son;
You are to get ready, yes, get excited,
For the best is yet to come!"

Reflection: I wrote this poem for a wonderful man of God. This man was going on to new challenges in Christ. The word the Lord gave me was that he had been blessed thus far, but the Lord said to tell him, **"The Best Is Yet To Come!"**

SPECIAL OCCASION

"To every thing there is a season, and a time to every purpose under the heaven" (Eccles. 3:1)

EVERYTHING BEAUTIFUL!

The Word of God says, to everything there is a season;
And under heaven a time; to every purpose and reason.
This is the time to praise, laugh, and embrace;
And be oh so grateful, for the Lord's amazing grace.
Consider what the Lord has done, you will find;
He has made everything beautiful in its time!

Whatsoever God does, it shall be forever, I know;
He has ordained this marriage union; His blessings will flow.
Uniting two lives into one, behold and see;
God has made these two lives, a one-flesh entity.
Consider what the Lord has done, you will find;
He has made everything beautiful in its time!

God's miracle of miracles, Jesus Christ the Son;
Just as He and the Father are, He has made you one.
Your God hath set eternity, in your heart;
Praise God; He has given you such a wonderful start!
Consider what the Lord has done, you will find;
He has made everything beautiful in life, in its time!

Reflection: A very special friend of mine was getting married. She is a beautiful and gifted sister in Christ! She asked me to write a poem for her wedding. She was marrying a wonderful man of God. All I could think of was how God brought them together and what beautiful timing the Lord has. That same day, the Lord led me to Ecclesiastes 3 and showed me that in their lives, He had truly made **"Everything Beautiful"** in its time!

MAKE YOUR MARRIAGE ONE THAT WILL GLORIFY ME!

"There is only one foundation, it's that which Christ has laid;
The Lord Jesus died for you, on Calvary the price was paid.
This is vitally important, please listen and take stock;
My little ones, please build your house on the 'Solid Rock.'
The joining of two lives is indeed a beautiful mystery;
Make your marriage one that will glorify Me!

Two shall become one and I want you to see;
This has truly become one of life's great mysteries.
The relationship between Christ and His Church
Is one of selfless love;
The two of you remember
To set your affections on things above.
The joining of two lives is indeed a beautiful mystery;
Make your marriage one that will glorify Me!

As I have cherished those who proclaim that Jesus is Lord;
So cherish one another, walking in Christ in one accord.
I Am with you today on this your wedding day,
I will emphasize it again; listen to My Spirit say;
The joining of two lives is indeed a beautiful mystery;
Please make your marriage one that will glorify Me!"

Reflection: My dear precious friend was getting married. What an awesome impact she has had on my life and ministry. I praise God for her and for the sweet spirit in which she gives warmth and love to our God and to others. Ephesians 5 gives a pattern for a godly marriage and relationships. This poem was simply an admonition to my two dear friends from the Lord; **"Make Your Marriage One That Will Glorify Me!"**

WHAT CAN I GIVE TO JESUS?

What can I give to Jesus, what can I give to my Lord and King?
What can I give to Someone, Who gave me a reason for living?
What can I give to Jesus, to my God in heaven above?
What can I give to the One, Who has filled me with so much love?
What can I give to Jesus, He speaks calm and peace to my heart?
What can I give to my Friend, Who said we'd never have to part?
What can I give to Jesus, His joy He's imparted to me?
What can I give to You now Lord, and throughout all eternity?
What can I give to Jesus, Who said, I need only believe?
What can I give to the Giver, Who invites to come freely receive?

What can I give to Jesus, He made me a child of the King?
What can I give to the Music, Who gave me a new song to sing?
What can I give to Jesus, the Sweet Lily of the Valley?
What can I give to my Master, I was blind, thank God, now I see?
What can I give to Jesus, He's the Bright and Morning Star?
Who says, *"I love you dearly, it doesn't matter who you are."*
What can I give to Jesus, the Lord and Savior of my soul?
What can I give to the Healer,
Who has completely made me whole?
I've asked, *"Lord, what can I give You*
For your pardon so full and free?"
Yes, I clearly hear Your voice right now;
All You really want is me!

Reflection: Our Christian Fellowship was discussing our theme for the month. We said that our theme should be **"What Can I Give To Jesus?"** While driving home that night, that question turned over and over in my spirit. When I arrived at home, the Lord confirmed our theme with this poem.

GOD'S GIFT OF LOVE

As the showers of blessings fall from heaven above;
Remember to always cherish God's gift of love.
Every good and perfect gift comes from the Father of Light;
The gift brings warmth and joy,
And in your heart you know it's right.

When Christ died for the Church, He planted a glorious seed;
And in Him you will find, everything in life you'll need.
Trust in the miracle your God has performed for you;
For He has made you one with each other, and with Him too.

Be sure to esteem one another, with Christ as your Head.
And glorify your Heavenly Father by being Spirit led.
My prayer for you this day, and as the years go by;
That to the Holy One of Israel; you will continue to draw nigh.
And as your showers of blessings fall from heaven above;
Remember to always cherish your God's wonderful gift of love!

Reflection: I was asked to write another wedding poem. I began to think of what a wonderful gift God gives in allowing us to express love in a marriage relationship, with Him as the "*Source and Head*" of that relationship. Rain or water (which is a type of the Holy Spirit) refreshes, rebuilds, and restores. God continually pours out His showers of blessings and love upon us. My prayer for them was that as God poured out His blessings upon them, they would always remember to cherish **"God's Gift Of Love!"**

IT'S ENOUGH JUST TO KNOW THAT YOU DIED FOR ME!

Lord, I have so many questions about this life.
There are so many problems; there is unending strife.
There are so many things in understanding I fail to see.
Yet in the depths of my heart, I know that You hold the key.
But as I begin to reflect upon the endless ages of eternity;
It's enough just to know that You died for me.

Now I don't know what makes the world go round.
Or what makes the birds sing such a beautiful sound.
Or what causes the trees to grow so strong and tall.
I also don't know what makes the snow or rain to fall.
Yet as I reflect upon eternity;
It's enough just to know that You died for me.

As I gaze up at the heavens and the magnificent starry sky;
I begin to think to myself and ask the question *"Why?"*
Why did You hang those stars up there so bright?
And how did You create such a glorious sight?
But as I reflect upon eternity;
It's enough just to know that You died for me.

Lord, what about the moon so clear, giving such brilliant light;
Creating such a heavenly glow on a warm summer's night?
And what about that wonderful soft and gentle breeze;
That gently sways the leaves, and gently bends the trees?
But as I reflect upon eternity;
It's enough just to know that You died for me.

Well, I guess the greatest mystery is my Savior's love.
It seems as deep as the ocean, wide as the sky above.
Dear Jesus, I must ask; why did I have any worth;
That You should sacrifice just to give me new birth?
I don't really understand, I only know
That when I reflect upon eternity;
My Lord, my God, it's more than enough
Just to know that You died for me!

Reflection: Another Passover season was approaching. I was very burdened with problems and the cares of this life. But I wanted to do something special for the Lord to let Him know how much I loved and appreciated Him. So I began to say to the Lord, *"I don't want to focus on anything, but the great sacrifice Jesus made for me."* I don't understand many things about this life, but the one thing I do understand above all else is Christ's love for me. **"It's Enough Just To Know That You Died For Me!"**

LOVE HAS BLOSSOMED IN GOD'S OWN TIME!

God has His times and seasons, we don't always understand;
Yet it's glorious to see the revelation, of the *"Master's plan."*
Just as a song unfolds, in rhythm, and in rhyme;
Love has blossomed, in God's own time!

Praise the God of heaven and earth, for all the joy He brings;
For the good and perfect gifts He gives, we let our praises ring!
The Father has united your hearts, in perfect harmony;
Consider how precious it is, it's one of life's great mysteries!
Christ's relationship with the Church,
Is one of sincere, pure love;
Your covenant will reflect this;
As your direction comes from above.
And as Christ has given life to,
And cherished the Church, for all eternity;
Cherish one another and glorify His name,
For all the world to see.

God has His times and seasons, we don't always understand;
Yet isn't it glorious to see the revelation, of the *"Master's plan?"*
Just as a song unfolds, in rhythm, and in rhyme;
Love has blossomed, in God's own time!

Reflection: When God joins two people together the result is so precious. It makes such beautiful harmony, just like a song. So it was in the lives of my two dear friends. God has His times and seasons in all of our lives, and for them; **"Love Has Blossomed In God's Own Time!"**

Psalms 16:11

Thou wilt shew me the path of life: in thy presence is fulness of joy; at thy right hand there are pleasures for evermore.

Made in the USA
Monee, IL
10 April 2021